ILLUSTRATED BY ROBERT GALSTER

THE BOOK OF HOLIDAYS

THE BOOK OF
HOLIDAYS

J. WALKER McSPADDEN

THOMAS Y. CROWELL COMPANY · NEW YORK

The following acknowledgments are made for permission
to reprint portions of poems:

"Johnny Appleseed" by Rosemary and Stephen Vincent
Benét, from *A Book of Americans* (Rinehart & Company,
Inc.), copyright © 1933 by Rosemary and Stephen Vincent
Benét, by permission of Brandt & Brandt.

"My Ireland" by Francis Carlin, copyright 1917 by J. F.
MacDonnell, by permission of Henry Holt and Company,
Inc.

"Sound of the Trumpet" by Fania Kruger, by permission
of the author.

"To Bolivar" by Rafael Pombo, translated by Alice Stone
Blackwell, from *Some Latin American Poets,* by permission
of the University of Pennsylvania Press.

Published in Canada by
Fitzhenry & Whiteside Limited, Toronto
Manufactured in the United States of America
Library of Congress Catalog Card No. 58-12464
ISBN 0-690-15224-8
FIRST PUBLISHED 1917
12 13 14 15 16 17 18 19 20

PREFACE

HOLIDAYS NEVER grow old, but books about them do. New holidays keep coming along; old holidays sometimes take on a new and added significance. To keep abreast of these changes we have prepared this completely new edition of *The Book of Holidays,* originally published in 1917, and revised in 1927 and 1940.

Holidays are tokens of devotion to some person or event or cause. The story of all the holidays ever celebrated in the world would serve as a rough outline of what man has found important and desirable through his recorded life on the earth. Our American holidays alone, some of whose roots go far back into history, tell a great deal not only about us but about the people of the entire world, whose tradi-

v

tions have traveled down the years and from country to country.

In a country as large as ours there are bound to be regional differences of opinion as to which holidays should be celebrated, and it is interesting to see how the states line up in these matters. Of the many days, state and national, in the greatly enlarged "A List of United States Holidays" at the back of this book, only seven are celebrated by all the forty-eight states: New Year's Day, Washington's Birthday, Independence Day, Labor Day, Veterans' Day, Thanksgiving, and Christmas. The three other most popular days, as measured by state observance, are Columbus Day, Lincoln's Birthday, and Robert E. Lee's Birthday.

Some high points of our recent history can be traced by the new holidays created since this book's last edition in 1940. Veterans' Day, November 11, though not a new holiday, has been greatly widened in scope. As Armistice Day, its former name, it honored the men of our armed forces who fought in the First World War; now it honors also the men who saw service in the Second World War and in Korea.

Armed Forces Day, the third Saturday in May, has replaced the former Army Day in April, Air Forces Day in September, and Navy Day in October. And Citizenship Day, formerly I Am An American Day, seems to carry a new dignity with its new name. V-J Day, August 14, although a legal holiday in only two states, is a date memorable for us all, marking the 1945 victory in the Second World War.

United Nations Day, October 24, is celebrated by all the eighty-one countries that are members of the United Nations, for the purpose of telling people everywhere what the UN has done and hopes to do.

Pan-American Day, celebrated on April 14, is one of the most significant holidays to have evolved in our contemporary history. A full chapter is devoted to it here, along with the holidays of Latin America.

Also, in this new edition we have given a full chapter to the Jewish New Year, Rosh Hashanah, and the other Jewish holidays so widely celebrated in this country.

CONTENTS

ix

NEW YEAR'S DAY

Ring out, wild bells, to the wild sky,
  The flying cloud, the frosty light:
  The year is dying in the night;
Ring out, wild bells, and let him die.

Ring out the old, ring in the new,
  Ring, happy bells, across the snow:
  The year is going, let him go;
Ring out the false, ring in the true.

From Section CVI, "In Memoriam"
by Alfred Tennyson (1809–1892)

Nᴇᴡ ʏᴇᴀʀ'ѕ ᴅᴀʏ has not always been the first day of January, though it is hard for us to think of it in any other season. For a very long time it was an early spring, rather than a winter, holiday. Time wasn't reckoned then as it is now, by the movement of the earth around the sun, and ancient peoples thought that the new cycle began with the first green of spring. Even when calendars were invented, there were at first only ten months instead of twelve, so that the Old Roman New Year fell on the first day of March.

When Julius Caesar, in 46 ʙ.ᴄ., introduced a new and better calendar, the two new months of January and February came into being for the first time. January, as you probably know, was named for the Roman god Janus, whose name in turn came from *janua,* the Roman word for "door." This god was always pictured with two faces, one looking backward, one forward; and January, like the door, swings both out and in. All the customs of New Year's Day, from ancient times right up to the present, have been connected in some way with bidding good-by to the past and welcoming a new and better future. Men have always longed for a new beginning and greeted it with joy when it comes. No wonder, then, that New Year's is the most universal, the most hopeful of all the holidays. It is only right that it should be at the head of a book, as well as at the head of the year.

Julius Caesar's calendar, called in his honor the Julian Calendar, was revised in A.D. 1582 by Pope Gregory XIII. This calendar, the Gregorian, adopted by England and the American colonies in 1752, is the one we use today. The way these calendars, each one improving on the one before, have brought the year to its present exact monthly divisions would be an interesting study in itself. You might also like to discover the difference between our "solar calendar" and the "lunar calendar" still used in some countries, based on the movement of the moon, rather than of the earth around the sun. If we tried to go further with these investigations here, this might become a Book of Calendars instead of Holidays! That book we will leave for one of you to write some day.

We know nothing about the very first New Year celebrations, for there were no records then. By the time of our first records, the festivities had become highly organized and elaborate, and the first festival we hear of took not one day but eleven days. This is believed to have begun about three thousand years before Christ, and was held in the temple at Babylon. The description of it, written in wedge-shaped characters on clay tablets, comes from Mesopotamia, to the north of Babylon. The ceremonies praised the native gods, who were identified with the sun and other heavenly bodies, and also served to purify the Babylonian people themselves for the new and better year to come.

This idea of purification, a kind of natural and spiritual housecleaning, has come down through the centuries in many different parts of the world. We are accustomed to bells ringing out the old and ringing in the new; but at one time sticks were also used, and the years were beaten out and in. It was thought that real physical help should be given the incoming year, to make sure that it would live up to expectations. For instance, to help along the apple harvest, boys in some English villages still go out early on New Year's Day to beat the apple trees with willow rods and sing this very ancient song:

> *Stand fast, bear well, top!*
> *Pray God sends us a howling crop;*
> *Every twig, apples big;*
> *Every bough, apples enow;*
> *Hats full, caps full,*
> *Full quarter sacks full.*

These boys are called "howlers," because they ask for a howling (big) crop. The "full quarter" means a quarter of a hundredweight. Sometimes the trees are also sprinkled with cider, to remind them of their ultimate duty.

Our own New Year's Day customs are well known to us. First there is the great combined Good Night and Good Morning given to the two years as they pass each other at midnight on New Year's Eve; a greeting so noisy in some places, as Times Square, New York, that nobody in the packed crowd can "hear himself think." At that moment there is no need for individual thought: all thoughts are the same—a slight sadness for Auld Lang Syne, but wild excitement at one more new beginning.

Both on the Eve and on the Day we indulge in the old, old custom of "Wassail." This universal toast comes from the old Gaelic words, *was hael,* meaning "good health," and signifies the special food and drink with which we wish each other well at this time. In Scotland and northern England wassail cakes and wassail bowls are still called by that name. We probably never called it wassail here, but for many years in the South, in New York City, and elsewhere there were all-day, open-house New Year's Day receptions. Although this gracious custom is no longer observed in quite the same way, hospitality is still the first rule of this holiday, and at eggnog parties, which are very popular, the great tradition of the bowl is carried on.

No songs are more endearing than the old wassail songs. There are many of them, but perhaps the most familiar is this one that poor children used to sing as they went from house to house, hoping for gifts of food. It has now become just a yearly serenade by neighborhood children. Though snow be on the ground they sang, and sing, the old familiar words:

> *Here come we a-wassailing,*
> *Among the leaves so green;*
> *Here we come a-wandering,*
> *So fair to be seen.*

The reason for the green leaves may possibly be that this, like so many New Year's customs, comes down from the time when New Year's Day was in the spring.

Everything that happened in the first hours and days of the year was of great import, and in many places still is. The first water drawn from the well, the "Cream of the Well," would stay fresh all year. The first twelve days predicted the weather for the twelve months. And "first-footing" had the greatest significance of all. The first person over one's threshold on New Year's morning was the "first-foot" and determined the luck of the year. This belief still continues in several countries. A dark man is good luck; a fair man just the opposite. A woman, either dark or fair, has always connoted death, but probably most women are too tactful to show themselves so early in the day. Also, since it is considered very risky to go out of the house until a first-foot has come in, it is strange that anyone ventures out at all.

These ideas would seem to put great hazards in the way of the New Year's visits for which the day has always been famous. So we are not surprised to read that sometimes people of the right specifications are hired, to be on the doorstep bright and early. The first-foot is, they say, better received if he also brings a gift: a bottle of whisky will insure his welcome in Scotland, but in Macedonia (showing how widespread is the habit) the visitor brings a stone, symbolizing strength, or a green twig, meaning life, and places it upon the hearth. Once in a while a member of the family takes it upon himself to be a proxy first-foot, going out and coming in again quickly and early, to forestall difficulties later.

An entire book, instead of a chapter, could be written on the omens and rituals of New Year's Day throughout the ancient and modern world. The Jewish New Year, as widely celebrated in our country as elsewhere, will be described later, in a chapter given over to Jewish holidays.

LINCOLN'S BIRTHDAY

And how shall I deck my song for the large
sweet soul that has gone?

From "When Lilacs Last in the Dooryard Bloom'd"
by Walt Whitman (1819–1892)

Four score and seven years ago...

THERE ARE still nineteen Southern states that do not celebrate Lincoln's Birthday. But everybody who does celebrate it makes up for several who do not, so great is the affection of those who love Lincoln. Although we wish we could have seen him and spoken with him, we feel almost as close to him now as if he were living. Everyone whose family ever came in touch with Lincoln feels proud. One woman has since childhood thought of him as "Mr. Lincoln" because her grandmother spoke of him that way, as if he were a close friend or neighbor; the child did not know that he was the President.

Some people are greater than the offices they hold or the great things they do. It is not just as a President that we know Lincoln, but as a great and loving man, a friend. The funeral train bore Lincoln's body through the country for two weeks after his death, and crowds gathered at every station to pay tribute to him. This popular feeling for Lincoln still continues. We know almost everything there is to be known about him, and yet we never know enough. Books and plays and poems about him are still being written, and probably always will be. Sometimes a prominent man is called "The Man of the Hour"; and, at the time that slavery was abolished and the Union held together, Lincoln was that man. But he is also the man of all hours. As Edwin M. Stanton, Secretary of War in Lincoln's Cabinet, said as he stood by his deathbed: "Now he belongs to the ages."

You probably already know about Lincoln's early life, but it is interesting to read what he himself wrote of it.

I was born February 12, 1809 in Hardin County, Ky. My parents were both born in Virginia, of undistinguished families—second families, perhaps I should say. My mother, who died in my tenth year, was of a family of the name of Hanks. My father, at the death of his father, was but six years of age, and grew up literally without any education. We removed from Kentucky to what is now

Spencer County, Ind., in my eighth year. We reached our new home about the time the State came into the Union. It was a wild region, with many bears and other wild animals still in the woods. There I grew up. There were some schools, so-called, but no qualification was ever required of a teacher beyond "readin', writin', and cipherin' to the rule of three." If a straggler supposed to understand Latin, happened to sojourn in the neighborhood, he was looked upon as a wizard. There was absolutely nothing to excite ambition for education. Of course, when I came of age, I did not know much. Still, somehow, I could read, write, and cipher to the rule of three, but that was all. I have not been to school since. The little advance I now have upon this store of education I have picked up from time to time under the pressure of necessity.

If any description of me is thought desirable, it may be said that I am in height six feet four inches, nearly; lean in flesh, weighing, on an average, one hundred and eighty pounds; dark complexion, with coarse black hair and gray eyes—no other marks or brands recollected.

His honesty, his modesty, and his humor may all be found in these direct and friendly words. When we read his speeches, we marvel even more at this "little advance" he said he had upon the store of education, for he was one of the finest speakers of all time, and his speeches and writing belong to the world's best literature. But that God-given power of expression is not to be gained, though it may be fostered, by education.

In 1818, two years after they had moved to Indiana, his mother died, and in 1819 his father married Mrs. Sally Johnson, the fine woman who Lincoln later said had been the guide of his life and had taught him all he knew about the Bible. The other books, few but important, which he had while he was growing up and which, as we know, he read at night by the pine-knot fire, were *Pilgrim's Progress, Robinson Crusoe,* Aesop's *Fables,* a history of the United States, and Weems's *Life of Washington.*

In 1830, when he was twenty-one, the family packed up again and, walking beside the oxen-drawn wagons full of household goods, over mountains and through swamps, they came to a spot on the Sangamon River, ten miles from Decatur, Illinois, where they built another home. And after Lincoln had seen his father and mother settled there, and had split enough rails to enclose their ten acres of land, he left them and set out alone for the unforeseeable years which lay ahead of him.

A trip that Lincoln took down the Mississippi River on a flatboat, in the summer of 1831, was the turning point of his life. A Springfield, Illinois, merchant hired him and his uncle and stepbrother to take a boatload of corn, pork, and pigs down to New Orleans. (Pigs are a hard cargo to handle and at one point he had to pick them up in his arms to get them aboard.) They built the flatboat themselves, loaded it, and started down the Sangamon, which would take them to the Illinois River and thence into the Mississippi. But when they came to the dam at New Salem, Illinois, the boat was too low in the water to cross it and they had to spend a day there adjusting the load. The trip in itself would have been a wonderful experience for him, but it was the day in New Salem that proved to be the important thing for Lincoln. The people of the village came down to the wharf to get acquainted with the unexpected visitors, and Lincoln liked them all so much that after the trip was over he went there to live.

It was during the six years he was there that his public life began. He held just about every position there was—clerk, county surveyor, and postmaster —as well as being partner in a grocery business. When the Black Hawk War came along he quite naturally got into it and was made captain of a company. This was the war, from June, 1831, to August, 1832, in which the Sauk and Fox Indians under Chief Black Hawk fought the United States in an attempt to regain their land east of the Mississippi.

And in 1832, at the age of twenty-three, Lincoln started on the road to the White House, as a candidate for the state legislature. He was defeated in this first try but in 1834 was elected, and for the three terms following, until 1841. Nowadays it often happens that a man is a lawyer before being elected to the legislature; but Lincoln didn't begin to study law until the year he was elected. Often he had to walk twenty miles to get the law books, which were loaned to him by John T. Stuart of Springfield.

It was also in New Salem that Lincoln met Ann Rutledge, who would have married him had she lived. Her death, in 1·835, during their engagement, was a great grief to him and for several years he had no further thought of marriage. But in 1837 a new life opened up for him. That was the year that he became a lawyer and moved to Springfield to live. Soon Lincoln had a busy practice. In 1842 he married Mary Todd, whom we now know as Mary Todd Lincoln. They had four sons, only one of whom, Robert Todd Lincoln, later minister to England, lived to grow up. But in the first part of the White House years a younger boy called Tad, a great favorite of his father's, was still with them.

Lincoln was a member of the United States House of Representatives from 1847 to 1849, and then for five years he left politics, rising to great prominence as an Illinois circuit-riding lawyer. In 1856 he became identified with the newly formed Republican Party and received 110 votes for the vice-presidential nomination on the Frémont ticket of that year. He was never in the United States Senate, for when he and Stephen A. Douglas contested a seat from Illinois in 1858, Douglas won. But the remarkable speeches that Lincoln made in seven famous debates with Douglas at that time so impressed the country that in 1860 he was nominated at the Republican National Convention for the Presidency of the United States, and the following November was elected. When he traveled from Springfield to Washington, D.C., in February, 1861, everyone flocked to the stations to see him, greet him, hear his voice and his words—a joyous trip in contrast to the sad journey home four years later.

Those last four years of his life were the years of the Civil War, or, as it is called in the South, the War Between the States or the War of Secession. Lincoln had left no doubt in the mind of the country as to how he stood on slavery: in the convention speech he made after being nominated for the Senate he said, "A house divided against itself cannot stand; I believe this government cannot endure permanently half slave and half free," and he said the same thing in other ways again and again in the debates. The Southern states, therefore, when he was elected, prepared for war and, on April 12, 1861, less than six weeks after his inauguration, Fort Sumter, in Charleston Harbor, South Carolina, was fired upon by Confederate forces.

The progress of the war itself you have read of elsewhere. Lincoln's proclamation freeing five million slaves was issued on January 1, 1863, with its famous last sentence: "And upon this act, sincerely believed to be an act of justice, warranted by the Constitution upon military necessity, I invoke the considerate judgment of mankind, and the gracious favor of Almighty God."

He was chosen President for a second term in November, 1864. On April 15, 1865, just six days after the war ended with the surrender of General Lee at Appomattox, the life of the President also came to a close. The evening before, as all the world knows, John Wilkes Booth, a man from a well-known family of actors, shot President Lincoln as he sat with Mrs. Lincoln and friends in a box at Ford's Theatre, Washington, watching the play, *Our American Cousin*. Having played his last part and made himself inglorious forever, Booth jumped to the stage and escaped, temporarily, by a stage door. Lincoln died at seven o'clock the next morning without having regained consciousness.

After its long journey through the country, already spoken of, Lincoln's body was laid to rest in Oak Ridge Cemetery in Springfield. Of this remarkable journey, Walt Whitman wrote in his poem, "When Lilacs Last in the Dooryard Bloom'd":

With the show of the States themelves as of crape-
    veil'd women standing,
With procession long and winding and the flambeaus
    of the night,
With the countless torches lit, with the silent sea of
    faces and the unbared heads,
With the waiting depot, the arriving coffin, and the
    sombre faces,
With dirges through the night, with the thousand
    voices rising strong and solemn,
With all the mournful voices of the dirges pour'd
    around the coffin,
The dim-lit churches and the shuddering organs—
    where amid these you journey,
With the tolling tolling bells' perpetual clang,
Here, coffin that slowly passes,
I give you my sprig of lilac.

In his Second Inaugural Address, only a few weeks before his assassination, Lincoln spoke of the job ahead, to bring the country together again in harmony. Certain words of that speech we all know: "With malice toward none; with charity for all; with firmness in the right, as God gives us to see the right, let us strive on to finish the work we are in; to bind up the nation's wounds; to care for him who shall have borne the battle, and for his widow and his orphan—to do all which may achieve and cherish a just and lasting peace among ourselves and with all nations."

This address is cut into the marble walls of the Lincoln Memorial in Washington, D.C., where the figure of Lincoln sits surrounded by his own great words. Also inscribed there is the Gettysburg Address, that brief talk he made at the dedication of the battlefield on November 19, 1863. He had had no time to prepare it; a few notes, only, were scribbled on a piece of paper. But always when Lincoln began to speak, something happened; no notes were needed; and on that day there came from his lips one of the most perfectly formed pieces of literature in existence. Many of you know it by heart:

Four score and seven years ago our fathers brought forth on this continent a new nation conceived in liberty and dedicated to the proposition that all men are created equal.

Now we are engaged in a great civil war testing whether that nation, or any nation so conceived and so dedicated, can long endure. We are met on a great battlefield of that war. We have come to dedicate a portion of that field as a final resting-place for those who here gave their lives that that nation might live. It is altogether fitting and proper that we should do this.

But, in a larger sense, we cannot dedicate, we cannot consecrate, we cannot hallow this ground. The brave men, living and dead, who struggled here, have consecrated it far above our poor power to add or detract. The world will little note nor long remember what we say here, but it can never forget what they did here. It is for us the living rather to be dedicated here to the unfinished work which they who fought here have thus far so nobly advanced. It is rather for us to be dedicated to the great task remaining before us—that from these honored dead we take increased devotion to that cause for which they gave the last full measure of devotion—that we here highly resolve that these dead shall not have died in vain, that this nation under God shall have a new birth of freedom, and that government of the people, by the people, for the people, shall not perish from the earth.

On Lincoln's Birthday, 1914, ground was broken for the Lincoln Memorial, and these words were engraved on the memorial. On Memorial Day, 1922, the finished building was dedicated.

SAINT
VALENTINE'S DAY

Good morrow! 'tis St. Valentine's Day
  All in the morning betime,
And I a maid at your window
  To be your valentine.

From "Hamlet"
by William Shakespeare (1564–1616)

The IDEA has never died that the first person seen on Valentine's Day will be one's valentine. That was why Ophelia, even in her madness, wanted to be "betime" at Hamlet's window on that day. (Perhaps you yourself sometimes take a quick glance out of the window that morning?) Shakespeare knew the custom in the sixteenth century; how much older it is we do not know, though it is possible that this is one of the customs that date from ancient Rome.

What is this very special holiday, which has a fragile but enduring quality all its own, and which seems to have no connection with Saint Valentine, the martyred Christian saint? Well, actually, it is two days thrown into one, the merging of a pagan and a Christian feast. Many of the customs of Valen-

27

tine's Day are from pagan times, but the name is Christian. In ancient Rome, when wolves were a great menace, there was a god called Lupercus, corresponding somewhat to the Greek god Pan, who kept the wolves away. And in his honor there was a festival, called Lupercalia, every fifteenth of February, at which young people always drew lots for game partners for the year. Later, when Valentine, a priest in Rome, killed about A.D. 270 during the persecution of the early Christians, was canonized, or made a saint, his feast day was established on the fourteenth of February, and the two days were combined. And very likely it was the time of year, when birds are nesting and new hope springing, that brought about the choosing of what came to be called one's "valentine."

England and France, and later the United States, have been the great Valentine's Day countries. The writing of valentines in both French and English has been a pastime and an art, a kind of light decoration in the field of love poetry. Valentines have even been written in prison: Charles, Duke of Orléans, taken prisoner in 1415 at the battle of Agincourt, composed some beautiful valentines while in bondage. In England valentine writing was at one time organized along orderly lines: *The Complete Valentine Writer,* published in London as late as the early nineteenth century, provided models of valentine composition for every kind of suitor in terms of his calling.

The first practice was to send gifts rather than verses, though a verse, or at least a motto, went along with it. Later the verse itself became the valentine. The custom of giving lavish presents was followed in certain circles and in certain periods—for instance, in the time of Charles II, from 1660 to 1685, when the ladies drew the gentlemen's names in Valentine's Day lotteries. There was a certain Duke of Richmond, Samuel Pepys tells us in his remarkable *Diary,* who, when drawn by a Miss Stuart as her valentine, gave her a jewel worth four thousand dollars. The next year (this drawing, as in Roman days, was a yearly occurrence) she was not quite so lucky, receiving from the next gentleman (probably not a duke) only a fifteen-hundred-dollar ring. Mr. Pepys himself gave a lady who drew him some very practical things: green silk stockings, garters, and shoelaces! And Mrs. Pepys, who once actually drew her own husband as a partner, had from him a ring "made of a Turkey stone set with diamonds," which sounds like a very nice gift indeed, though what a Turkey stone is must be left to our imagination.

Charming Valentine's Day superstitions have abounded. In 1756 a young girl wrote: "Last Friday was Valentine's Day, and the night before I got five bayleaves, and pinned four of them to the four corners of my pillow and the fifth to the middle; and then, if I dreamed of my sweetheart, Betty said we should be married before the year was out. But to make it more sure, I boiled an egg hard, and took out the yolk, and filled it with salt; and when I went to bed, ate it shell and all without drinking or speaking after it." The really important thing—whether she did dream of the sweetheart—she does not tell us. There is always the chance that digesting the eggshell may have brought a nightmare instead. Who can say?

Another odd and delightful thing they did in those days was to get up before the sun and try to snare an owl and two sparrows. What was it they were after? Wisdom and modesty, for use in their future love lives? Or aren't sparrows modest? It is hard to believe they ever caught these creatures; but if they did, it meant good luck for the rest of the year.

The hideous and usually unkind valentines miscalled "comic" now seem to be outmoded, and there is more and more a return to what we think of as truly and typically a valentine: lacy, delicate, and full of a genuine hope and affection. Cupids, arrows, bleeding hearts, ancient as they are in their symbolism, can still convey the message that we mean. And, since valentines are supposed to be always anonymous, there's no reason to feel silly about it.

WASHINGTON'S
BIRTHDAY

February—you are very
  Dear, when all is done:
Many blessings rest above you,
You one day (and so we love you)
  Gave us Washington.

From "Washington-Month"
by Will Carleton (1845–1912)

Washington's Birthday was celebrated not only during his lifetime but also before he was President. Without his generalship there might never have *been* a presidency, and it is good to know that it was as a general—in the year 1782, while the Revolution was still being waged—that he was first honored in this way. The first mention made of such a celebration was in that year, when the *Virginia Gazette,* evidently a weekly, reported, "Tuesday last being the birthday of his Excellency, General Washington, our illustrious Commander-in-Chief, the same was commemorated here with the utmost demonstrations of joy." It was, as it happened, his fiftieth birthday, a fine time for this kind of recognition. And the next

35

year, with a big banquet in New York for which great preparations were made and special songs written, it was agreed that the Washington's Birthday celebration would thenceforth be an annual event.

Then came victory. The British troops having evacuated New York, the 1784 celebration there was a very special one, and the first official celebration of the day on record. The occupation was over; the city belonged to itself, and so did the country! A New York newspaper, in the fine, controlled speech of the time, said that the day "was celebrated here by all the true friends of American independence and constitutional liberty with that hilarity and manly decorum ever attendant on the sons of freedom. In the evening an entertainment was given on board the East India ship in this harbor to a very brilliant and respectable company, and a discharge of thirteen cannon was fired on this joyful occasion." It is wonderful to imagine being one of that brilliant company, with Washington himself probably present, and hearing the cannon, thirteen of them in one concerted roar. There is still a great reverence for Washington's Birthday, which is a legal holiday in every state, but the first tremendous excitement belonged to the lucky people alive that night.

From that time on the celebrations multiplied so

swiftly that before the year of Washington's death, 1799, there was hardly a town too tiny to manage a ball or a banquet, for without dancing or feasting, or both, the day was not complete. The parties had, so far as possible, the same courtly dignity that Washington himself exemplified. After his death the celebrations went on in steadfast thankfulness for his life and its inestimable significance for us.

Washington was sixty-seven when he died, on December 12, 1799, two days after having caught cold while making the usual rounds of his plantation on horseback. The trouble is now believed to have been acute laryngitis; the treatment given him was bloodletting. He knew that he could not recover, and the last things he said are entirely characteristic of him. "I die hard," he said, "but I am not afraid to go. I believed from my first attack that I should not survive it. My breath cannot last long." A little later he said, "I feel myself going. I thank you for your attentions; but I pray you to take no more trouble about me. Let me go off quietly. I cannot last long." He instructed his secretary about his burial, felt his own pulse, and quietly died. A very great gentleman, calm, capable, considerate of others, he died as he had lived.

How true were the words that Thomas Jefferson

wrote of him later: "He was indeed a wise, a good and a great man. His integrity was most pure; his justice the most inflexible I have ever known. He was incapable of fear, meeting personal dangers with the calmest unconcern."

Washington was born in Westmoreland County, Virginia, on February 22, 1732. His life was a busy, active one from the start, and he had a certain flair for hardship, being always strong, intrepid, and adventurous. Also, he always had a gift for war, as a boy dividing his playmates into two armies, himself at the head of the American, and a chap aptly named William Bustle at the head of the "French," which then meant the enemy. Every day, with cornstalks for muskets and gourds for drums, the two amicable armies would turn out, march, and fight; cooperating almost as a unit.

His first school is believed to have been a little old field school kept by a man named Hobby, one of his father's tenants who acted both as sexton and schoolmaster. Washington, though reputedly no great scholar, was always good at mathematics. His last two years in school were in fact devoted to engineering, geometry, trigonometry, and surveying; and at sixteen, in 1748, he was appointed a public surveyor. This job took him into the wilderness and kept him there intermittently for some years. Says one authority, he was "engaged to survey these wild territories for a doubloon a day, camping out for months in the forest, in peril from Indians and squatters." But actually it seems that the backwoodsmen and the Indians all liked him very much, and he liked them. Also, the pay was good. "A handsome salary," one man calls it. And even if the doubloon had then gone down from its original value of sixteen silver dollars to the five it eventually reached, the cost of living in the forest wasn't high. Incidentally, his surveying knowledge came in handy much later when, in 1791, as President, he himself determined the boundaries of the new "Federal City" (later Washington, D.C.) and the location of its public squares.

When George was nineteen he was made a major in charge of one of the military districts into which the colony of Virginia was divided for handling attacks on the frontier by French and Indians. This was the real beginning of the seven-year French and Indian War. Two years later he was sent on a mission to the French, to find out just what their intentions were and to warn them off. This meant six hundred miles alone through the wilderness. But for a young fellow of his build, experience, and aptitudes this was all in the day's work and probably very enjoyable. In 1754 he commanded a regiment against the French, who had established themselves at Fort Duquesne (now Pittsburgh); but he was driven back by superior forces to Fort Necessity, the American stronghold, which he held as long as humanly possible before surrendering. In 1755 when General Braddock led two regiments of volunteers against Fort Duquesne, Washington went along as aide to the general. In this campaign he received four bullet holes in his coat and had two horses shot under him; but he came out safely, the only aide left alive. There was still work ahead of him.

Washington's home had for years been with his older half-brother Lawrence at his estate, Mount Vernon, on the Potomac River. Their father, Augustine Washington, had died when George was twelve years old. When Lawrence died in 1752 he left Mount Vernon to George, whose home it remained all his life. Mount Vernon is now a beautifully restored national shrine. After his marriage to Mrs. Martha Custis in 1759 and until the Revolution began, Washington lived as a doubly busy country gentleman, managing both her estate and his own. Mrs. Custis was a widow with two children, John and Martha Parke Custis; and they and, later, their children made up to Washington for the children he himself never had. After the war, he was able to settle down at Mount Vernon again for some years. In 1789 he left for New York, where Congress was sitting and where the first President of the United States was to live through his two terms of office. That triumphal trip up through New Jersey, a state he knew so very well during the trying war years, was an interesting one. At Elizabethtown (now plain Elizabeth) he embarked on a splendid barge which was followed by other barges and boats, making a long water procession reminiscent of Elizabethan times, up the Bay of New York.

The inauguration, on April 30, was at Federal Hall at the corner of Nassau and Wall Streets. This beautiful building, later known for many years as the Subtreasury Building, reverted to its original name in 1939 and is now the Federal Hall Memorial. Look at that corner now any day at noon, and you'll think it couldn't ever have been more crowded; but on that day of the inauguration of our first president, it *was* more crowded, with no break in the great mass of faces as far as sight could reach. The General had become the President, and for ten more years, eight in office and two at home, would hold the welfare of his country in his heart and in his capable large hands.

SAINT
PATRICK'S DAY

My Ireland is mine in truth
    For all the saints who clung to Her;
The patriots who died in youth,
    And the harpers who have sung to Her.
The holy saints who clung to Her,
The harpers who have sung to Her,
My Ireland is mine in truth
    Because I would be hung for Her.

From "My Ireland"
by Francis Carlin

THE SEVENTEENTH of March was not the day
Saint Patrick was born, but the day he died. His
birthday is not known, but his birth year is placed by
modern Catholic scholars as A.D. 385, and the
year of his death as A.D. 461. This makes him
seventy-six years old when he died, and not well
over a hundred, as the legends have it.

It was through this beloved patron saint that Ireland became one of the great Catholic countries,
and so closely is he identified with the country that
March 17 is Ireland's greatest national holiday as
well as holy day. Wherever Irish people live, the day
is known for high spirits and deep feeling, a colorful, joyful occasion which nobody wants to miss.

This great festival of national and religious devotion and nostalgia isn't just "a great day for the Irish," but for all of us. Have you ever watched a New York City Saint Patrick's Day parade go flowing up Fifth Avenue, hour after hour? The whole city takes on a greenish cast. And not to wear a bit of the green, even if your ancestors never set foot on the Auld Sod, would be hardly civil.

Saint Patrick's life is so thickly strewn with loving legends that separating the historical from the imaginative has been, and still is, a big job for the researchers. Legend, also, spreads much faster than fact. We have all heard that Patrick drove the snakes out of Ireland. Many of us have read how the sun refused to set for twelve whole days and nights after he died, but stood perfectly still so as not to bring a new day without him. But relatively few of us know the actual facts of his life which are gradually being discovered. Says the writer Francis X. Weiser in *The Holyday Book:* "It will take many more years before Saint Patrick's figure emerges with some degree of certitude as the 'real Patrick,' freed from later additions. However, much has been found already, and these historical details make the Saint so wonderfully alive, so touchingly great, that not even the wildest legends could render him more attractive."

Patrick's family, Roman citizens though Breton Celts in race, had an estate on the west coast of England. As a boy of sixteen, Patrick was captured by some Gaels (Irish) who were raiding the coast and taken to Ireland, where for six years he was held a slave, tending sheep. But finally he managed to get aboard a boat bound for the Continent with a cargo of Irish hounds; and so at the age of twenty-two he reached France and thence made his way home to his family.

But something about Ireland had impressed itself upon him and when he made up his mind to study to be a missionary, it was the Gaels whom he wished to convert. He traveled for a while in Italy, Gaul (France), and some islands in the Tyrrhenian Sea, but then settled down to study for the priesthood, under Saint Germanus, the Bishop of Auxerre in France. Finally, in the spring or summer of A.D. 432, after many years' preparation and after he had become a bishop himself, Patrick reached Ireland to begin the tremendous work of conversion and Church organization which never ceased during his lifetime. When he died, he was Archbishop and Primate of the See of Armagh, which he had founded in his later years.

The twenty-nine years of his labors were not easy ones. The people themselves, the Gaels whom he had come to know so well as a boy, did not greatly oppose him and his mission. It was the Druids who didn't want Christianity. They were an ancient group of Celtic sorcerer-priests regarded by many people nowadays as practically mythical, but really at that time very much alive and very powerful. They were a remarkable class of people, including bards and prophets, and combining the offices of priest, physician, wonder worker, and judge. Naturally they did not want that power questioned. This was perhaps the hardest fight Christianity ever had to make against the thought and customs of the ancient world. But one of the legends about Saint Patrick is that he himself was of the Gaelic (Irish) race; and no wonder they thought so, for he was a fighter equal to themselves. And in the end he won.

Saint Patrick's Day has always had an agricultural significance in Ireland, too. It is the day when the stock are driven out into the pastures for the summer. "Saint Patrick turns the warm side of the stone uppermost," as the old Irish saying has it, and farmers still start planting their potatoes on that day. The

very earth of Ireland, the crops and cattle, follow
him.

But the legends have a value of their own, sup-
plementing history. The things that are made up
about a man as time goes on tell so much about the
kind of person he was, to inspire such love and trust.
We now know that Saint Patrick didn't use the tre-
foil shamrock to illustrate the doctrine of the Holy
Trinity, but that doesn't make the precious symbol
any the less right and true. All good things, poetic
and picturesque, the Irish people lay now at his
door. And feeling like this is catching. That is why
so many thousands of those little fabric shamrocks
are sold along the streets of America on Saint Patrick's Day in the morning.

PAN-AMERICAN DAY

LATIN-AMERICAN HOLIDAYS

TO BOLÍVAR
by Rafael Pombo

Thou fillest all of South America;
From the Atlantic shore to Potosi,
No snake, no brier that did wound thy feet,
No palm that did not wave to honor thee.

Here, thy last antagonist is Time.
Thy triumph waxes as the years decay;
For even our errors and our meannesses
Make thee stand out still greater every day.

Translated by Alice Stone Blackwell

PAN-AMERICAN DAY we have in common with the
Latin-American countries. This holiday has been
observed by the twenty-one American republics
since 1931. The date, April 14, goes back to the
first International Conference of American States
in 1890, at Washington, D.C., when the International
Union of the American Republics, now known as the
Organization of American States, was created. The
Pan-American Union, with a building of its own in
Washington, is the General Secretariat of the or-
ganization. The member states are Argentina,
Bolivia, Brazil, Chile, Colombia, Costa Rica, Cuba,
the Dominican Republic, Ecuador, El Salvador,
Guatemala, Haiti, Honduras, Mexico, Nicaragua,

Panama, Paraguay, Peru, the United States, Uruguay, and Venezuela.

The whole idea of American solidarity began much longer ago. In 1815, Simón Bolívar, the military liberator of South America who is now called the father of the Pan-American movement, set down his vision for the future of America in what is known as the "Jamaica Letter." "More than anyone," he said, "I desire to see America fashioned into the greatest nation of the world, greatest not so much by virtue of her area and wealth as by her freedom and glory." And in 1826 the Congress of Panama, or "Great American Assembly," established, as Bolívar said, "the plan of the first alliances that marked the beginning of our relation with the universe." The one hundred thirtieth anniversary of that Congress was marked in 1956 by the Panama meeting of American presidents and the O.A.S. Council.

In 1948 the Charter of the organization was signed, giving authority to principles and policies long in the making. Article 4 outlines its aims: "a) To strengthen the peace and security of the continent; b) To prevent possible causes of difficulties and to ensure the pacific settlement of disputes that may arise among the Member States; c) To provide for common action on the part of those States in the event of aggression; d) To seek the solution of political, juridical and economic problems that may arise among them, and e) To promote, by cooperative action, their economic, social and cultural development."

To carry out this ideal of development, teachers, engineers, architects, agronomists, doctors, and other professionals from all countries are pooling their knowledge and experience to provide the 347 million people of the member states with more and better schools; better crops and food supply; better health, housing, city planning, transportation, industry, and trade.

Pan-American Day is celebrated largely by young people in schools with special entertainments, usually folk songs and dances—the pleasantest way of coming close to the customs of other countries. It is always interesting to see how we ourselves stand among the nations. The little booklets of song and dance which the Pan-American Union publishes for use in Pan-American Day programs are not big enough to include all countries every year; but we find the United States in one such fascinating little collection represented by "Skip to Ma Lou," one of the well-known "play-party" square dances of our southern mountains. ("My" is spelled "Ma," to give the local pronunciation.)

Also, young people from the various member

countries make trips to the Pan-American Union in Washington during Pan-American Week, April 8–14, giving entertainments of their own. The choir and band of Boys' Town, Monterrey, Mexico, for instance, stopped off there recently on a concert tour, very picturesque indeed with their instruments and big-hatted, short-jacketed costumes. A fiesta in the Union's patio brought together the charming customs of several different countries; and girls from a Virginia school took part in a musical program in the more formal Hall of Americas.

Radio programs, too, are sometimes given on this day. One such broadcast was made in 1956 by young people representing the four languages and cultures of the continent: a girl from the United States speaking English, one from Brazil speaking Portuguese, and two boys, from Haiti and Argentina, speaking, respectively, French and Spanish.

Another day that we share to a certain extent with the Latin Americas is October 12, but with them it is not only Columbus Day or Discoverer's Day, but also the Day of the Race (Día de la Raza). This is a peculiarly Latin-American holiday, honoring the Spanish heritage of the people of Latin America. The big cities celebrate it by speeches, parades of school children, and in other conventional ways;

but in areas of large Indian population it is the occasion of colorful fiestas, sometimes lasting several days. In Guayaquil, Ecuador, a temporary village is built on the outskirts of the town, where the celebrators live during the festivities so that the spirit of holiday may not be broken by ordinary activities.

There is also a celebration called the Day of the Indian (Día del Indio), which begins on June 24 and actually lasts a whole week. These festivities, especially in Peru, preserve and present the old native customs, music, and folklore. People flock from all over the country to enjoy dancing, poetry, musical contests, horsemanship exhibits, sports, and general feasting, in the time-honored leisurely Indian fashion.

All over Central and South America the revolt against Spanish rule came to a head between the years 1810 and 1825. The days of liberation of the various republics, different in each country, are as important as our Independence Day. Also, July 24, the birthday of the great liberator Simón Bolívar, is very generally celebrated, though the city of Caracas, Venezuela, where he was born, considers the holiday particularly its own. In Mexico, March 21 is an honored day: the birthday of Benito Juárez, the full-blooded Indian who was president of that country from 1858 to 1863 and again from 1867 to 1872, and protected Mexican rights against enemies both without and within. This holiday is affectionately called "The Day of the Indian Child."

On Corpus Christi Day, the Thursday after Trinity Sunday, observed in honor of the Sacrament of the Lord's Supper, Indians from remote mountain regions move in solemn procession carrying their sacred images, as one onlooker has said, with "touching primitive sincerity."

Christian festivals are observed as in all Christian countries, with the difference that the converted Indians have often grafted their old pagan customs onto the traditional usages brought by the Spanish conquistadores.

Epiphany, January 6, the Feast of the Three Kings, is an especially beloved religious holiday. For one thing, it is the day on which gifts are given to children, as Christmas is with us. Shoes are left on the window sill to be filled, and grass is also left there to feed the camels of the Three Kings, who have carried the gifts so far. It is a long trip to have made, but fortunately they arrive in summer weather, when refreshment is plentiful.

Carnival is the gay, glad period just before Lent, into which enough merriment and fantasy must be packed to last through the forty fasting days to come. In Ecuador sham battles with paper bags full of perfumed water or fine flour make Carnival hazardous for visitors—some of whom have even been seen sheltering themselves under umbrellas. In Panama, Carnival takes on a more formal aspect. Women wear exquisitely embroidered costumes decorated with finest lace, and the national dance, the *tamborito,* displays these dresses to advantage as they whirl and twirl. Masquerades, balls, parades with extraordinary floats, beautiful dark-eyed señoritas —all these things which we associate with southern romance—blossom out luxuriantly during Carnival.

Besides the fixed holidays of these fiesta-loving countries, there are many other annual times of joy and excitement which have more flexible dates: Chile's famous rodeos in July, August, and September; the Cattle Fair at Buga, Colombia, in July; and the various harvest festivals and fairs. And, in thinking of all this, we must remember that our sister states are half a globe away, and when it's autumn here, it's spring there. The Day of the Race, for instance, on the same date as our Columbus Day— when October is beginning to be nippy in our part of the world—is often combined with a spring festival. Between us all, we keep the year very busy.

GOOD FRIDAY

EASTER

THE WORLD ITSELF

The world itself keeps Easter Day,
   And Easter larks are singing;
And Easter flowers are blooming gay,
   And Easter buds are springing.
     Alleluia, alleluia.
The Lord of all things lives anew,
And all His works are living too.
     Alleluia, alleluia.

by John M. Neale (1818–1866)

THE CHRISTIAN CHURCH keeps its own calendar. The Christian year begins with Advent, which is the season of the preparation for Christmas, the celebration of Christ's birth; and reaches its peak with Easter, the great festival of joy at Christ's resurrection.

Easter has no fixed date, but there is a fixed way of finding when it will come each year. In A.D. 325 the astronomers of Alexandria, Egypt, experts in calculating dates that depended on the course of heavenly bodies, were authorized by the Council of Nicaea to help the Archbishop of Alexandria determine for the whole Church the date of Easter. They came up with an answer which has served for sixteen hundred years. Easter is celebrated on the first Sunday following the full moon that appears on or after the vernal equinox, about March 21. The Easter dates for 1959 through 1970, for example, are:

1959	March	29	1965	April	18
1960	April	17	1966	April	10
1961	April	2	1967	March	26
1962	April	22	1968	April	14
1963	April	14	1969	April	6
1964	March	29	1970	March	29

Lent, the forty days' fast in remembrance of Christ's fast in the desert, precedes Easter as Advent precedes Christmas. Originally it began on Sunday. But since the fast did not apply to Sundays, in the seventh century Pope Gregory set the beginning of Lent back four days to the preceding Wednesday, to make the period of fasting exactly forty weekdays. So began the observance of Ash Wednesday, initiating the season of repentance and of preparation for Good Friday and Easter, Christ's death and resurrection, the two days that are at the heart of the Christian religion. As Francis Carlin, an Irish poet of this century, has put it very simply in his poem, "The Greatest Feast":

The greatest Christian feast by far
—Since Christmas only has a star—
Is Easter with its sun, without
Which Christmas would be dark as Doubt.

Good Friday is now observed as a legal holiday by eleven states: Connecticut, Delaware, Florida, Lousiana, Maryland, Minnesota, New Jersey, North Dakota, Pennsylvania, South Carolina, and Tennessee; and by five counties in Arizona. In states that do not keep the holiday such as New York, business firms usually give time off to employees who wish to attend the three-hour service which is held from twelve to three in many churches.

The original Good Friday on which Christ died was also the Jewish Passover (from the Hebrew word *Pesach*). It was the Passover feast that Christ and His disciples had observed the night before, and to which Christ gave a new significance. It might be said that here the two faiths met, and also diverged, one growing from the other. It was on Passover that the Pascal lamb was sacrificed; but for Christianity, Christ Himself was the lamb or sacrifice.

As are all spring festivals, Easter is also closely tied to the nature worship of the ancient world, through customs and legends still surviving. The word "Lent" is in fact believed by some authorities to have come from the old Anglo-Saxon, *Lengtentide,* season of lengthening days. The Norsemen had a word, *Eostur, Eastur, Ostara,* or *Ostar,* which meant season of the growing sun, and from this comes our *Easter.*

There are certain customs so associated with Easter that we just take them for granted. But why, for instance, are rabbits supposed to bring the eggs? What have eggs, anyway, to do with Easter? Why do we color them, hide and hunt them, roll them down the White House lawn? Well, it all goes back to the fertility lore of spring. The egg looked as dead as anything could be, but it carried life inside. The rabbit, being the most prolific of animals, also represented fertility. The old customs were taken over with new meaning by the Christians, when new life came to the spiritual as well as to the natural world. The egg tradition has grown and flourished. In Slavic countries especially, elaborate decoration of eggs has for many years been an art form in itself.

Certain legends have also woven themselves around the days of Holy Week preceding Easter. There is an ancient story still alive among Roman Catholic children that eggs are brought not by rabbits but by bells, which fly to Rome after Mass on Holy

Thursday to fetch the eggs which on their return they drop into children's homes. As no Mass is held and no bells are rung for the rest of the week after Holy Thursday, it is reasonable to think that the bells may be away. While in Rome they sleep on the roof of St. Peter's.

In many little towns of Sussex, England, old men and boys play marbles on Good Friday, before and after services. Because they play on the ground beside the church gate it is thought that this was at first an imitation of the soldiers throwing dice at the foot of the Cross, for Christ's robe. Another curious custom, not so easily explained, was followed in Brighton, England: the whole village of fishermen skipped rope on Good Friday. Perhaps this signifies some kind of fellowship with the Apostles who had once been fishermen.

Shrove Tuesday, the day before Ash Wednesday and therefore the last day of carnival before the fast, is actually a legal holiday in three of our southern states: Louisiana, Florida, and Alabama. In New Orleans the Mardi Gras (Fat Tuesday) celebration is especially famous. The ancient carnivals of which this is a lively souvenir were originally designed to drive winter away.

Of course we all know about hot cross buns:

Hot cross buns, hot cross buns,
One a penny, two a penny,
Hot cross buns.

They cost more than that now, but we all eat them. But in ancient times they were something more than sweet and delicious—they had magical powers. If you ate them on Good Friday itself, your home would not catch fire in the next year. And if you feared other disasters, you hoarded them—in sickness they would serve as medicine, and if worn as charms they would ward off shipwreck and other unfortunate occurrences.

The custom of taking an "Easter Walk" through fields and country after church on Easter still continues in some parts of Europe. And though the tremendous number of Fifth Avenue paraders in New York, who fill the street from curb to curb for many blocks, carry no crucifix or lighted candles as people do in the Easter Walk, still the same Christian joy is expressed in both customs. Everybody dresses up for Easter, wherever he is, but it isn't only the wish to show off fine new clothes that brings everybody out. It is the irresistible urge, as old as Christianity, to celebrate in company with one's neighbors this great day of the Christian year when Christ rose from the dead.

MAY DAY

SONG: ON MAY MORNING

Now the bright morning-star, day's harbinger,
Comes dancing from the east, and leads with her
The flowery May, who from her green lap throws
The yellow cowslip and the pale primrose.
Hail, bounteous May, that dost inspire
Mirth and youth and warm desire!
Woods and groves are of thy dressing,
Hill and dale doth boast thy blessing.
Thus we salute thee with our early song,
And welcome thee, and wish thee long.

by John Milton (1608–1674)

MAY DAY was the "maddest, merriest day" of Merrie England, and it began early. The custom was for everyone to go out into the woods a little after midnight, so as to get back by dawn, bringing with them the great sprays and branches of the may, or hawthorn, a prickly tree with pink and white blossoms, related to the rose. As Alfred Noyes tells in his ballad, one special prank was for the Lord of Misrule and all his court to come trooping up the aisle of a church where services were being held, dancing, singing, and waving garlands high above their heads.

But it wasn't only to church they went. They left flowers at the homes of friends—a custom we still follow, in hanging May baskets on the door—and the culminating event of the day was the dance around the Maypole. This was no small Maypole, such as the ones the school children of America dance around in parks, but a huge and ancient veteran of the forest which took forty yoke of oxen to transport. Getting it into the ground was no easy job and when it got there it usually stayed for the whole year, until another giant took its place. Little booths and arbors were often built around it, and it became the center of something like a fair.

No holiday has had a stronger hold on people's love of fantasy and spring merrymaking. England was not the place of its origin, though there it reached its peak. As have so many festivals, it comes down to us from ancient Rome, from a celebration in honor of Flora, the goddess of flowers and the spring. Children twined garlands around the marble columns of her temple, and laid them on the altar. The *flamen florialis,* or priest of Flora who received their offerings, wore a long white mantle, a tall, conical white cap trimmed with wool and topped with olive wood, and the olive wreath of his order. The first boy or girl to lay a garland on the altar was the lucky one until the next May Day. After making their offerings, they all danced the flower dance, a stately minuet, in honor of the goddess and her day.

That was a long time ago but May Day still goes on, and so does the dancing, right here in America. In New York City, for example, there are five celebrations by school children, one in each borough. These Park Fetes, as they are called, do not come on May Day itself, but on five different days through the month. And there is always an alternate date set for each of them, to allow for bad weather. The celebration in 1957 was a notable one, being the fiftieth anniversary of this Maypole festival of the New York City schools.

For this golden jubilee the poles were gilded, and gold balloons floated from their tops. Winding the many-colored streamers around them were over twelve thousand children, and the remarkable thing to onlookers at any one of the Fetes was how children from so many different schools, without any rehearsal together, blended so perfectly into one great unified company. The dances are representative of various places and cultures. For this fiftieth anniversary they were the "Csehbogar," "La Raspa," Buffalo Gals," "Patty-Cake Waltz," "Seven Steps," the square dance "Red River Valley," the Swedish "Gustaf Skoal," the American square dance, "The Girl I Left Behind Me," and, at the end, the old traditional "Maypole Dance," to the Elizabethan tune of "Bluff King Hal."

In England, May Day was also, for some reason,

the chimney sweeps' own day. Their chosen representative, called "Jack-in-the-Green," almost invisible amid the branches he was dressed in, had a prominent place in the great procession which moved in formal but lively fashion to the Maypole. This great train of merrymakers also included the milkmaids, complete with cow and milkpail and, in the late eighteenth century and later, Robin Hood and his Merry Men. Nor was England alone in these celebrations. May has always had much the same response in different countries. France's little Queens of the May personified the Virgin Mary, to whom the month of May belongs. German lads, they say, were never satisfied with branches alone but planted whole trees before their sweethearts' windows. In almost every land, in fact, the tribute of the forest green was offered up to the beloved month of May.

In many places, too, the dew which falls during that night and early morning is supposed to have special properties of beauty and blessedness. Girls bathe their faces in it, and people in many regions still walk barefoot through the woods and fields to obtain the healing powers of the dew.

Back in the 1880's, May Day was also significant in this country as a time for labor demonstrations in connection with the big struggle then going on for the eight-hour day. In October, 1884, a group of trade unions later known as the American Federation of Labor set May 1, 1886, as the date from which "eight hours shall constitute a day's labor." On the day designated, a strike was called, backed not only by these trade unions but also by left-wing and revolutionary groups. Many cities were involved, with Chicago as the strike center. Out of this strike developed the "Haymarket Riot," in Haymarket Square, Chicago, a demonstration held on May 4 at which a bomb was thrown, killing seven policemen. Eight anarchists were found guilty, four of whom were hanged. Those who went to prison were later pardoned by Governor John Peter Altgeld of Illinois, who believed the trial had been unfair.

This May Day, very much more turbulent than any which the Lord of Misrule could have devised, was never repeated. May 1, in 1890, was chosen as the date for reinaugurating the campaign, and this time a nation-wide strike was planned. But in 1889, President Samuel Gompers and other leaders of the American Federation of Labor succeeded in limiting the strike movement, and when the day came it was only the carpenters' and other building trade unions which struck. May 1, 1889, was also celebrated as the first International May Day by Marxist labor groups in European countries.

Since the riotous May Days of the 1880's, May

Day has been observed in this country chiefly as a holiday with games and pageants, but even this custom has been gradually dying out. Although the European Labor May Day is still celebrated by Socialist and Communist groups, labor in the United States now has its own day. You will read about it in a later chapter.

ARBOR DAY
BIRD DAY

Why did he do it?
We do not know.
He wished that apples
Might root and grow.

He has no statue.
He has no tomb.
He has his apple trees
Still in bloom.

Consider, consider,
Think well upon
The marvelous story
Of Appleseed John.

From "Johnny Appleseed 1775–1847"
by Rosemary and Stephen Vincent Benét

IT IS a strangely exciting thing to plant a tree or to see one planted. Nobody who ever shared in a school Arbor Day tree-planting will forget the feeling of witnessing an act of importance, a solemn transaction between oneself and the earth. Putting flower seeds or seedlings into the ground is satisfying and good, but does not have the sense of long-range venture that comes as the spade cuts into the turf and a new tree is set for better or for worse into its own permanent place of growth. Every tree is a personality and, like a child, will become a unique being in its own right. We can keep on watering it for a while, but it will go its own way. We can give it a name (every Arbor

Day tree is named for someone) but that name will be forgotten. Trees need no names.

The tree-planting crusade in this country had its beginning in 1872 in Nebraska, the region which at one time in geography books was marked "The Great American Desert." A far-seeing citizen, J. Sterling Morton, pointed out that the thing to do would be to plant trees over those great barren prairies, and he suggested that a certain day be set apart each year when everybody could join in the planting. A lot of people laughed at the idea of trees ever growing on those plains. But Mr. Morton was right—they did grow, and now this is excellent agricultural country, full of flourishing farms and orchards. In 1895 the state legislature even resolved that Nebraska should be known as the "Tree Planters' State," a well-deserved title, for more than a million trees were planted the first year, and since that time nearly a billion. The State Board of Agriculture, which offered prizes for the counties and persons planting the largest number of trees, was largely responsible for this tremendous achievement.

The actual Arbor Day movement for schools was begun by B. G. Northrup, chairman for many years of the American Forestry Association. He initiated the idea of schools setting aside a certain day each spring for planting trees, and suggested giving a dollar to every boy or girl who planted, or helped to plant, five trees. That was back in the 1860's and 1870's, and now Arbor Day is observed in every state. There is no one date for Arbor Day, for climates and conditions vary too greatly throughout the country, but it is usually early in May.

The whole idea of tree planting stems, of course, from the need for reforestation. As President Theodore Roosevelt said in an Arbor Day letter to the school children of the country:

A people without children would face a hopeless future; a country without trees is almost as hopeless; forests which are so used that they cannot renew themselves will soon vanish, and with them all their benefits. A true forest is not merely a storehouse full of wood, but, as it were, a factory of wood, and at the same time a reservoir of water. When you help to preserve our forests or plant new ones you are acting the part of good citizens.

This need for reforestation is now thoroughly understood by everyone and is being constantly met by the government. The Civilian Conservation Corps, which was created by Act of Congress in June, 1937, and functioned until 1943, served to make this steady work of renewing forests more widely known than ever before. During a period of financial depression and widespread unemployment, CCC (Civilian Conservation Corps) camps were established throughout the country to provide work for young men in forestry.

Although Arbor Day itself is not very old, the custom of planting trees is ancient. In the older parts of the world, long experience brought wisdom about the value of forests, and trees were closely bound up with human living. The ancient Aztecs of Central America, centuries before Columbus sailed to these shores, are said to have planted a tree every time a child was born, the tree taking the same name as the child. Indians in some parts of Mexico still keep this custom. In Germany, where careful forestry is traditional, families have a tree-planting ceremony forty days after Easter.

But aside from the obvious economic necessity of perpetuating healthy tree life, there is our esthetic need—the love we have for trees, the place in our happiness that only they can fill. One great gift that Arbor Day brings to the young generations of children is the joy of a greater knowledge of trees, of their differences and their individual beauties. Johnny Appleseed, that odd and wonderful character who tramped the country in the early 1800's with sacks full of seeds for sowing, specialized in apple trees.

Perhaps each of us has one especial favorite: oak or elm or maple, sycamore or larch or pine. But each tree is lovely, and different, with its wonderful gift for

> *Annihilating all that's made*
> *To a green thought in a green shade,*

as Andrew Marvell, an English poet in the seventeenth century, said.

Interesting ways of observing Arbor Day have sprung up in many states. In Mississippi and Texas, it is part of Conservation Week. In Connecticut there are two Arbor Days, one in April and one in October —a sensible solution, since some trees do better if planted in the fall. And in the eight states of California, Connecticut, Delaware, Georgia, Illinois, Massachusetts, Tennessee, and Wisconsin, Arbor Day is also Bird Day.

Bird Day has no fixed date, but almost everywhere falls in May, the great bird month. The purpose of Bird Day, as of Arbor Day, is largely conservation. The beauty of birds, as they dart and stop and swoop, would seem reason enough for their existence; but birds serve other ends, too. They literally save the farmer's life by destroying the insects that destroy the crops. A passage from *Bird Life,* by Dr. Arthur Michler Chapman, sums up their work in arresting fashion:

In the air swallows and swifts are coursing rapidly to and fro ever in pursuit of the insects which constitute their sole food. When they retire the nighthawks and whip-poor-wills take up the chase, catching moths and other nocturnal insects which would escape day-flying birds. Flycatchers lie in wait, darting from ambush at passing prey, and with a suggestive click of the bill returning to their post. The warblers, light, active creatures, flutter about the foliage, and with almost the skill of a humming-bird pick insects from the leaf or blossom. The vireos patiently explore the under sides of leaves and odd nooks and corners to see that no skulker escapes. The woodpeckers, nuthatches, and creepers attend to the trunks and limbs, examining carefully each inch of bark for its eggs and larvae, and excavating for the ants and borers that they bear within. On the ground the hunt is continued by the thrushes and sparrows, and other birds. Even the insects which pass their earlier stages or their entire lives in the water are preyed upon by the water birds.

In many states Bird Day is arranged in connection with the National Association of Audubon Societies, whose object is the protection and preservation and photographing of wild birds in their native haunts.

MOTHER'S DAY
FATHER'S DAY
CHILDREN'S DAY

I'll to thee a simnel bring,
'Gainst thou go'st a-mothering,
So that when she blesseth thee,
Half that blessing thou'lt give me.

From "To Dianeme"
by Robert Herrick (1591–1674)

To "GO A-MOTHERING" in the late Middle Ages meant for young people who had to live away from home, apprenticed or in domestic service, to go home to visit their mother church. On that mid-Lent Sunday called Laetare Sunday, boys and girls also had a chance to see their own mothers, and they brought presents to them as well as to the altar. For the human mothers the special gift was the "simnel" cake of which Robert Herrick speaks in his poem. The observance of "Mothering Sunday" still persists in certain parts of England, and simnel cakes (plum cakes made of *simila,* fine flour) are still especially made and sold at that time, as the traditional gift.

People have always given the name "Mother" to

things that they reverenced most and held most dear: for example, Mother Jerusalem, Mother Church, and in mythology the various Mothers of the Gods. Mother's Day here in America, first celebrated in 1914, does not stem from the Laetare festival, but all holidays which carry the word "mother" in their names pay homage in a general way to the same idea, of home, origin, refuge. To return home bearing gifts is a most natural and universal act. We were a little late in giving a name to it, but surely people everywhere have always been taking trips home, symbolic or actual, with something corresponding to a simnel cake in their suitcase. "He who goes a-mothering finds violets in the lane" is an old saying that well suggests the sweetness of reunion.

On May 9, 1914, President Woodrow Wilson issued a proclamation directing officials to display the national flag on all government buildings, and asking the people, also, to hang out their flags on the second Sunday in May, as a "public expression of our love and reverence for the mothers of our country." In recommending such a holiday to the President, Congress spoke of the home as "the fountain-head of the State" and of mothers as influential for good government and humanity. Not only is the holiday usually celebrated on Sunday, but, in schools, on the preceding Friday, and often by civic organizations on Saturday.

The first Mother's Day was planned by a Philadelphia Sunday school, and from this the idea spread across the nation. The choice of pink and white carnations as Mother's Day flowers—pink to be worn for a living mother, white if the mother is dead—is said to have been made in memory of President William McKinley, who had always worn a white carnation, his mother's favorite flower.

The complement of Mother's Day is, of course, Father's Day, which falls on the third Sunday of June. President Calvin Coolidge recommended the national observance of this day in 1924, though President Woodrow Wilson had officially approved the idea as early as 1916. It is said that Spokane, Washington, was the first city to establish a Father's Day, in 1910. The rose is the official Father's Day flower—a white rose for remembrance, and a red rose as a tribute to a living father.

Children's Day, on the second Sunday in June, is observed in Protestant Sunday schools. The church service is usually given over to the children, who march in and fill the front pews. Many of them take part in the exercises, each class, from oldest to youngest, being represented. This day for children was started in 1868 by the Methodist Episcopal Church, and was gradually taken up by the other churches.

MEMORIAL DAY

ODE WRITTEN IN THE YEAR 1746

How sleep the brave, who sink to rest
By all their country's wishes blest!
When Spring, with dewy fingers cold,
Returns to deck her hallow'd mold,
She there shall dress a sweeter sod,
Than Fancy's feet have ever trod.

By Fairy hands their knell is rung,
By forms unseen their dirge is sung;
There Honour comes, a pilgrim gray,
To bless the turf that wraps their clay,
And Freedom shall a-while repair
To dwell a weeping hermit there!

by William Collins (1721–1759)

DECORATION DAY, its popular name, is the better designation for this holiday. A Memorial Day could be kept without flowers; a Decoration Day cannot, and this is the day we offer flowers to our soldier dead. Our recollections of the day—long-ago recollections of older people, recent recollections of the young—have to do not only with speeches and parades, but with the actual flowers laid upon the earth. Of course the wild flowers and garden flowers blooming around the thirtieth of May differ greatly in various parts of the country. There may be daisies, buttercups, black-eyed Susans, clover, and Devil's paintbrush; or yellow lilies, iris, and syringa from the borders and hedges. But in some places these flowers have either come and gone, or not yet arrived.

Although Memorial Day is a legal holiday in every state (except in Texas where it is only a bank holiday), it is not celebrated on May 30 in every state. There is a Confederate Memorial Day in certain Southern states, and this is celebrated on various days. In Florida, Alabama, Georgia, and Mississippi the date is April 26. Virginia calls May 30 Confederate Memorial Day. May 10 is the day in the Carolinas. And in Kentucky, Louisiana, and Tennessee it is June 3, the birthday of Jefferson Davis, who was President of the Confederate States of America from 1861 to 1865.

It was Southerners who first began the decorating of soldier graves. Two years after the Civil War, some women of Columbus, Mississippi, decorated the graves of both Confederate and Union men. This was such a fine and welcome gesture in those heartsore days that the custom spread and was made official. In May, 1868, General John A. Logan, Commander-in-Chief of the Grand Army of the Republic, issued an order naming May 30

as the day, for the purpose of strewing with flowers or otherwise decorating the graves of comrades who died in defence of their country, and whose bodies now lie in almost every city, village, or hamlet churchyard in the land. . . . It is the purpose of the commander-in-chief to inaugurate this observance with the hope that it will be kept from year to year while a survivor of the war remains to honor the memory of the departed.

No survivor of that war remains, but the memories of it grow longer—as do the parades, with floats and civic organizations and drum majorettes twirling their gay batons, and with lines and lines of young veterans from Korea and the Second World War, and shorter lines of older men who saw service in the First World War. Wars persist. We still decorate, and always will, the graves of the men whose bodies reach home. Even in the Civil War some did not. There was a poem, "Cover Them Over," by Will Carleton, about them:

Cover the thousands who sleep far away—
Sleep where their friends cannot find them today;
They who in mountain and hillside and dell
Rest where they wearied, and lie where they fell.

The custom of placing flowers upon graves is an old one, and exists in many countries. The Greeks had rites called *zoai* which were performed over each new grave. If the flowers took root and blossomed on the graves, it meant the souls were send-

ing back the message that they had found happiness.
The Roman festival, called Parentalia, or Day of the
Fathers, lasted for eight days in February—violets
and roses were the special flowers. Whatever the
flower, wherever the grave, this placing of flowers
upon graves has always seemed the natural thing
to do.

FLAG DAY

Flag of the free heart's hope and home,
By angel hands to valor given;
The stars have lit the welkin dome,
And all thy hues were born in heaven.
Forever float that standard sheet!
Where breathes the foe but falls before us,
With Freedom's soil beneath our feet,
And Freedom's banner streaming o'er us?

From "The American Flag"
by Joseph Rodman Drake (1795–1820)

THE POEM prefacing this chapter tells how a young man of the new republic felt about its flag. Joseph Rodman Drake, the poet, who was only twenty-five when he died in 1820, grew up with that young flag. He was born in 1795 when the final design of the Stars and Stripes was still undecided, and lived only two years after it had settled definitely into its present form. The ardor of his feeling has not been, could never be, equaled in any later work, though many other poems have been written about the American flag; and Drake will always be associated with the early days of "that standard sheet."

It was on June 14, 1777, that the Continental Congress adopted the original form of the flag. A

committee had been appointed, and this description
of the design was prepared:

The stars of the new flag represent the constellation of
States rising in the West. The idea was taken from the
great constellation of Lyra, which in the hand of Orpheus
signifies harmony. The blue in the field from the edges of
the covenanter's banner in Scotland, significant of the
league covenant of the United States against oppression,
incidently [sic] involving the virtues of vigilance, perseverance and justice. The stars are disposed in a circle
symbolizing the perpetuity of the union; the ring like the
serpent of the Egyptians, signifying eternity. The thirteen
stripes showed with the stars the number of the united
colonies, and denoted the subordination of the states to
the Union, as well as equality among themselves. The red
color in the Roman days was the signal of defiance, denoting daring; and the white, purity.

According to legend, the good committee, if left
to its own devices, would have given us six-pointed
stars; but Mrs. John Ross, upholsterer and seam-
stress, who was to make the flag, preferred a five-
pointed star, and with a few snips of the scissors she
showed the gentlemen how much trimmer the less
bulky stars would be—especially as their numbers
increased. The gentlemen of the committee were
Robert Morris, Colonel Ross (no relation to Betsy),
and perhaps even George Washington himself. And
they agreed that she was right.

Although Congress formally approved the new flag in 1777, it was two or three years before the flag was generally adopted. Until 1780, in fact, many flags of stripes only, and no stars, were in use, and Washington wrote in 1779, "It is not yet settled what is the standard of the United States." But naval vessels of the United States hoisted the new flag soon after its approval; and when the *Ranger*, commanded by Captain John Paul Jones, arrived at a French port on February 14, 1778, the flag received the first salute ever paid it by foreign naval craft.

With new states coming into the Union, a final decision about the flag had to be made. When Kentucky and Vermont were admitted in 1794, both stars and stripes were increased to fifteen. But in 1818 Congress voted to restore the original thirteen stripes, denoting the original states made from colonies, and to add a new star for each new state, on the Fourth of July following its admission. (The stars were by this time no longer in a circle.) This flag, now with forty-eight stars, is the one we know today: alternating red and white stripes with a blue field for the white stars. The admission of Alaska to the Union in 1958 will require a change in the design of the flag to include a forty-ninth star.

Betsy Ross was no newcomer to the field of flag

making. As is shown by an old bill paid by Congress the preceding year, she had already made flags for the Revolutionary War troops. There had been several of these regional wartime standards. In March, 1775, a red flag bearing on one side, "George Rex and the liberties of America," and on the other side, "No Popery," was flown in New York. *Rex* is the Latin word for king, and refers here to King George III. "The liberties of America" refers to the colonists' opposition to the taxes imposed on them. In July, 1775, General Israel Putnam raised a flag over his troops bearing the motto of Connecticut, "Qui Transtulit Sustinet," and on the other side, "An Appeal to Heaven." The motto "An Appeal to Heaven" also appeared on a white flag bearing a pine tree, carried by the vessels defending the Boston harbor. And the Virginia troops used a rattlesnake for their symbol, with the ominous words, "Don't tread on me," below it. Which of these, if any, were made by Betsy Ross, we do not know. If you have a free hour in Philadelphia some day, you may wish to visit her home, now a national shrine, at 239 Arch Street, one of the old residential streets of the city—the place where the first true Stars and Stripes is said to have come into being.

Like the flag itself, Flag Day did not reach its completed form at once. It was not until May 30,

1916, that June 14 was established as Flag Day by proclamation of President Woodrow Wilson. The date, of course, came from June 14, 1777, when Congress had adopted the design. But as early as June 14, 1897, New York State observed the day, when the governor proclaimed that on this anniversary the national flag should fly over all the public buildings of the state. Philadelphia also observed Flag Day that same year. Although Pennsylvania is the only state that keeps the day officially as a legal holiday, the other states observe it unofficially, by raising the flag at dawn on all public buildings and on many private homes.

There is an etiquette and courtesy about the use and handling of the flag that has become instinctive as well as traditional. When Francis Scott Key, during the War of 1812, wrote of seeing "by the dawn's early light" the flag that he had hailed at "the twilight's last gleaming," it was because it was wartime and during battle; only then may the flag fly after sunset or before sunrise. Also, when raised or lowered, the flag must not touch the ground or the deck of a ship, and it must be saluted by everyone present during the hoisting or lowering. When it is being placed at half-mast for the dead, it must be hoisted first to the top of the staff, then lowered into place. When it passes in parade, spectators should rise if sitting, stop if walking, uncover their heads, and stand at attention. When the flag is carried in parade with any other flag it has the place of honor, at the right of the other flag. If a number of flags are carried, it should either precede the rest by several paces or be carried in the center, above the others, on a higher staff. When it is displayed on the wall, the union (the field of stars) is at the flag's right. Nothing should ever be placed upon the flag or attached to it; and neither the flag nor any picture of it should be used for decorative or advertising purposes.

There is another young man, a Frenchman, General Lafayette, who, like the poet Drake, is associated forever with our flag. When he died in 1834, the state of Virginia shipped Virginia earth to France, that he might lie in American soil. And at the head of his grave is an American flag which has flown there continuously since his burial. As Lafayette's great-great-great-grandson, Count René de Chambrun, wrote after the Second World War: "During the long, dark years of German occupation, it may well have been the only American flag in occupied Europe, a secret spark of hope in the darkness."

INDEPENDENCE DAY

Quickly at the welcome signal
   The old bellman lifts his hand;
Forth he sends the good news, making
   Iron music through the land.
How they shouted! What rejoicing!
   How the old bell shook the air,
Till the clang of freedom echoed
   From the belfries everywhere.

From "Independence Bell"
Author unknown

THE OTHER day some boys were asked if they knew when Independence Day was celebrated. They gave it up, and on being told that it was July 4, one of them said, "Well, why didn't you *say* the Fourth of July, and be done with it?"

Yes, here is one holiday which is easy to remember if we use the popular name, and we are not likely to do anything else. Ever since that greatest of all July Fourths in our history, it has lived in our affections by this one name, and no amount of calling it "Independence Day" is going to change it. It is a legal holiday in every state in the Union—our one distinctive, universal, national holiday.

The Fourth of July is really the birthday of our

nation. It celebrates the first definite break of the American Colonies with Great Britain, when the Declaration of Independence was passed by the Continental Congress, in Philadelphia. The story of the events leading up to this historic act is well-known. Scattered hostilities had been taking place for several months. War against the mother country had been threatened unless certain oppressions should cease. Petitions were made. But still England would not regard the rights of the colonists seriously. In her eyes they were only rebels to be dealt with as seemed best to her statesmen. The colonists protested that they were not rebels but "petitioners in arms," and that they were willing to lay down their arms if their wrongs were righted.

After all this sparring for position, things began to move more quickly. Down in North Carolina and Tennessee a band of patriots had already formulated the Mecklenburg Declaration, renouncing all connection with England; and when the Continental Congress met in 1776, a strong sentiment for entire separation from the mother country was apparent. On June 7, Richard Henry Lee, of the Virginia delegation—instructed, he said, by the unanimous vote of the Council of Virginia—presented the following resolution: "That these United Colonies are, and of right ought to be, free and independent States; that they are absolved from all allegiance to the British Crown; that all political connection between them and the State of Great Britain is, and ought to be, totally dissolved."

John Adams of Massachusetts quickly seconded the motion. A debate of four days followed, as this was a very perilous matter for all of them, and then a committee was appointed to prepare such a declaration to this effect, setting forth the grievances that had brought it about. The committee consisted of Thomas Jefferson, Benjamin Franklin, John Adams, Roger Sherman, and Robert B. Livingstone. The actual writing of the Declaration is attributed to Thomas Jefferson; and although Jefferson made use of the phrases of others in its composition—reciting grievances which were on the lips of everyone—his literary skill and power of collecting ideas have made it one of the most incisive documents in the history of the world. The Declaration of Independence was completed and laid before Congress on June 28, and after another week of earnest debate, a few small changes were made, and it was accepted by Congress and signed by the President of Congress, John Hancock, in that full, bold signature so familiar to us all, on July 4, 1776.

On August 2, the engrossed copy now so carefully preserved in a lightproof safe at Washington, D.C., was formally presented to Congress and received the signatures of delegates from every one of the thirteen colonies. These were brave men. Their act meant that if the cause of the new nation should fail, every one of the signers could be convicted of high treason and put to death. As Franklin aptly put it, "We must all hang together, or assuredly we shall all hang separately."

While Congress deliberated on that first great Fourth of July, the streets of Philadelphia were thronged with excited men. Around the State House, where Congress was assembled, they had stood all day long, waiting for action on the momentous measure. All business was forgotten while the people pressed forward, all eyes fixed on the building and upon the belfry where the old bell ringer awaited the signal. The bell had been brought from England, but around its rim these prophetic words were cast, "Proclaim Liberty throughout all the land unto all the inhabitants thereof." And the bell ringer was hoping he could help it do just that.

And sure enough, that day it was to fulfill its mission. At two o'clock in the afternoon, after the long hours of waiting, the door opened. A boy ran out into the street waving his arms and shouting wildly to the bellman, "Ring! Ring! Ring!" And the famous Liberty Bell boomed out its message to the people.

Christopher Marshall, who kept a diary at this time called *Remembrancer,* states that four days later a more formal celebration occurred on a "warm sunshine morning" in the yard of the State House, "where, in the presence of a great concourse of people, the Declaration of Independence was read by John Nixon. The company declared their approbation by three huzzas. The King's Arms were taken down in the Court Room, State House." Then they went to the Commons, where the same was proclaimed to each of the five battalions. It was "a fine, starlight, pleasant evening. There were bonfires, ringing bells, with other great demonstrations of joy upon the unanimity and agreement of the Declaration."

The first military celebration of Independence Day was held July 9, under the direct orders of General Washington, who notified Congress of the event as follows: "Agreeably to the request of Congress I caused the Declaration to be proclaimed before all the army under my immediate command; and have the pleasure to inform them, that the measure seemed to have their most hearty assent; the expres-

sion and behavior, both of officers and men, testify-
ing their warmest approbation of it." The army's
approbation took more definite form later, for, as an
eyewitness relates, "last night the statue of George
III was tumbled down and beheaded, the troops having long had an inclination to do so, thought the time
of publishing a declaration of independence a favor-
able opportunity, for which they received a check
[demerit] in this day's orders." Each year thereafter
the day was celebrated by the army. The usual ceremonies were a salute of thirteen guns, the reading
of the Declaration, a double allowance of grog, and
the freeing of men confined in the guardhouse.

At the time of the signing of the Declaration,
John Adams wrote a letter to his wife, a letter that
has become historic. "I am apt to believe," he said,
"that it [the day] will be celebrated by succeeding
generations as the great anniversary festival. It
ought to be commemorated as the day of deliverance, by solemn acts of devotion to God Almighty.
It ought to be solemnized with pomp and parade,
with shows, games, sports, guns, bells, bonfires, and
illuminations, from one end of this continent to the
other, from this time forward forevermore." Never
have words proved more prophetic, to the smallest
detail. In fact, the Glorious Fourth became after a

while our most dangerous as well as most glorious day. Much later, when elaborate fireworks were banned, the words "safe and sane" also came into favor.

By a remarkable coincidence, Thomas Jefferson, the author of the Declaration, and John Adams, one of the signers and its great supporter, both of whom were afterward Presidents of the United States, died on the same day—Independence Day, 1826. On June 30 of that year someone asked John Adams, who was then very ill, for a toast to be given in his name on the Fourth of July. He replied, "Independence forever!" When the day came, hearing the noise of bells and cannon, he asked the cause and, on being told, murmured, "Independence forever!" Before evening he was dead.

LABOR DAY

Then let us pray that come it may,—
  As come it will for a' that,—
That Sense and Worth, o'er a' the earth,
  May bear the gree, and a' that.
For a' that, and a' that,
  It's coming yet, for a' that,—
That Man to Man, the warld o'er,
  Shall brothers be for a' that!

From "For A' That and A' That"
by Robert Burns (1759–1796)

LABOR DAY, the recognition of what its founder, Peter J. Maguire, called "the industrial spirit—the great vital force of every nation," has been for many years a legal holiday in every state. The wish of the American Federation of Labor in 1886, that "it shall be as uncommon for a man to work on that day as on Independence Day," very quickly came true. After the nation's first Labor Day parade on September 5, 1882, in Union Square, New York, Labor Day was observed every year, though it was not made a national holiday until 1894.

In the *American Federationist* (official monthly magazine of the American Federation of Labor and Congress of Industrial Organizations) for September, 1956, there is an illustration of that first parade. The drawing is a fine one, for *Frank Leslie's Illustrated Newspaper,* from whose issue of September 16, 1882, it was reproduced, did not pick its artists carelessly. Looking at it, we feel that we are there ourselves among the spectators lining the Square, watching the marchers swing up around the park. The shadows are falling slightly to the east, so it must be early afternoon. The ladies' parasols are raised, so we guess that it is warm. But there is a breeze from the west, which keeps the flags on all the buildings flying. And even if we didn't know the year, we can tell that it is the early eighties, for the ladies are wearing bustles.

From where we are standing, at the north end of the Square, we have an excellent view of the big signs that the marchers carry. "Vote for the Labor Ticket" has just passed us. "The True Remedy Is Organization and the Ballot" is directly in front of us. And coming toward us are "All Men Are Born Equal"; "8 Hours Constitute a Day's Work"; "Labor Creates All Wealth"; "Agitate, Educate, Organize"; and "Abolish Convict Labor." The others are still too far away to see, but they will reach us in a minute.

Fifteen years later, in 1897, Maguire, the founder of Labor Day, described how it all came about:

It was reserved for the American people to give birth to Labor Day. In this they honor the toilers of the earth and pay homage to those who from rude nature have delved and carved all the comfort and grandeur we behold.

More than all, the thought, the conception, yea, the very inspiration of this holiday came from men in the ranks of the working people—men active in uplifting their fellows and leading them to better conditions. It came from a little group in New York City, the Central Labor Union, which had just been formed and which in later years attained widespread influence.

On May 8, 1882, the writer made the proposition. He urged the propriety of setting aside one day in the year to be designated as "Labor Day" and to be established as a general holiday for the laboring classes. He advised that the day should first be celebrated as a street parade which would publicly show the strength and esprit de corps of the trade and labor organizations. Next the parade should be followed by a picnic or festival in some grove and the proceeds of the same divided on this semi-cooperative plan, viz:

Each union or organization should get as many tickets as it desired to sell: the more sold the greater would be the profits of the society selling them. Each society should be allowed to keep all the money realized by sale of tickets through its members. In the end each of the bodies participating should contribute to the expenses in proportion to its membership.

It was further argued that Labor Day should be observed as one festal day in the year for public tribute to the genius of American industry. There were other worthy holidays representative of the religious, civil and military spirit, but none representative of the industrial spirit— the great vital force of every nation. He suggested the first Monday in September of every year for such a holiday, as it would come at the most pleasant season of the year—nearly midway between the Fourth of July and Thanksgiving, and would fill a wide gap in the chronology of legal holidays. Many were the cogent reasons he advanced and at once the idea was enthusiastically embraced.

The first Labor Day Parade and festival of the Central Labor Union of New York City on September 5, 1882, was an imposing success. From that day on it became a fixed institution in the United States, observed today in every city of the land. The plan was next endorsed by the annual convention of the American Federation of Labor. . . . It spread rapidly from city to city and town to town. City councils and state legislatures took it up and made it a legal holiday, until finally, June 28, 1894, it became a national holiday by Act of Congress.

Mr. Maguire, a carpenter by trade and founder of the United Brotherhood of Carpenters and Joiners of America, was active in the American Federation of Labor from the very first, having written the call for the convention of trade unions at Columbus, Ohio, in December, 1886, which established the new federation. He was made successively secretary, second and first vice-president, and until 1900, six years before his death, was a member of the executive council. He and Samuel Gompers, President of the American Federation of Labor, were delegates to the British Trades Union Congress in 1895. And before this, when Maguire was delegate to the International Workingmen's Congress in Switzerland in 1881, he made a study of the economic conditions of European workers.

On every Labor Day the Philadelphia District Council of Carpenters make a pilgrimage to Arlington Cemetery, Camden, New Jersey, and hold memorial services at Mr. McGuire's grave.

Labor has marched a long way since that first Labor Day, but parades still come every year. This way of celebrating is permanent and popular. The day is still, as McGuire intended, a "festal" one, a long weekend for workers. Banners are not so much in favor as in the early days, but if they were, they would now carry messages of world-wide import, to fit the broadening problems and conditions that concern labor as well as everybody else. The eight-hour day has long been in effect; a thirty-hour week is now a possible goal; but Labor Day and the forces behind it are now not only protesting wrongs and demanding rights, but are acting with other citizens of this country for peace and prosperity.

Nothing changes so fast as industry, adapting its

skills to every new scientific and technological finding. This also means that labor must reconstitute its own organized life to fit modern needs. George Meany, President of the American Federation of Labor and Congress of Industrial Organizations, in an article in *Fortune* magazine, has taken a look ahead to the year 1980—a far cry indeed from that windy day in 1882!

In the years leading up to 1980, he said, "the form of collective bargaining will, as in the past, adjust to the changing structure and functioning of business itself. . . . The economics of the industry, the structure of the enterprise, and the scope of union recognition are the principal factors dictating the types of collective bargaining. . . . In the atomic-energy field, for example, where a multiplicity of crafts create bargaining problems, a new form has been evolved whereby craft workers are free to choose their own union, with bargaining conducted through a joint council." Meany foresaw that preparation for "automation," factories run entirely by electronic devices, meant "the establishment of severance pay, retraining of skills, reorganization of work schedules."

Labor Day is a holiday whose meaning grows with each year, for every year American labor shows more comprehension, skill, and adaptive power.

ROSH HASHANAH
(Jewish New Year)

OTHER JEWISH HOLIDAYS

SOUND OF THE TRUMPET

The Shofar, symbol of the new year, blows;
The tone resounds, and faithful mankind knows
It is the call of peace that's yet to be,
A long-drawn note of all humanity.

by Fania Kruger

Rosh Hashanah, the Jewish New Year, means "head of the year," and is observed at the beginning of Tishri, the first month of the Jewish year. It celebrates the anniversary of the creation of the world which, according to tradition, occurred in the year 3761 B.C. It is also considered the Day of Judgment, when all mankind is judged by the Creator, and the fate of each person for the coming year is written in the Book of Life. There is no fixed date on our calendar for Rosh Hashanah, since the Jewish calendar is determined by the movements of the sun and moon in relation to each other (a lunisolar calendar); it falls either in September or the early part of

125

October. The months of the Jewish year are Tishri, Heshvan, Kislev, Tebet, Shebat, Adar, Adar Bet or Adar Sheni (which occurs only in Leap Year), Nisan, Iyar, Sivan, Tammuz, Ab, and Elul.

Rosh Hashanah, the New Year, ushers in the most solemn period of the Jewish year, the ten days of self-examination and repentance which reach their fulfillment in Yom Kippur, the Day of Atonement. These ten days of penitence, or "High Holy Days," or "Days of Awe," differ from other Jewish festivals in that, though deeply traditional, they are neither historical nor agricultural, but concern each Jew as an individual rather than as a member of the group.

The observance of all Jewish holidays begins at sunset of the previous day. On the Eve of Rosh Hashanah in the homes, after the recital of the kiddush, or sanctification prayer, and the lighting of the festive candles, the head of the household dips food in honey and says, "May it be God's will to grant us a good and sweet year." At the close of the synagogue services that evening the worshipers greet each other with the time-honored New Year wish, "Leshanah tovah tekatevu vetehatemv," which means "May you be inscribed and sealed [in the Book of Life] for a good year."

The ancient and intricate ritual connected with

the blowing of the *shofar,* a trumpet made of a ram's horn, is followed in the synagogue services of Rosh Hashanah. The *shofar* is blown during the morning service before the Scroll is returned to the Holy Ark, and during the service later in the day. Sixty to a hundred sounds, arranged in various combinations, are blown, the exact number varying with different traditions. The sounds are of three kinds: a long deep note which ends abruptly, three broken notes, and a wavering sound consisting of nine short, broken notes. In ancient times the *shofar* was sounded to announce the days on which the new moon and the festivals would fall; every fiftieth year, to proclaim the Jubilee, when all Hebrews who were slaves were freed; to issue a call to battle; and to give tidings of a victory.

Yom Kippur, the Day of Atonement, is the most sacred day of the Jewish year. From sunset of the evening before until the fall of night the next day, the worshipers abstain from all food and drink. A taper large enough to burn for twenty-four hours is lighted in each home in memory of the dead. Petitions for forgiveness are made at the synagogue services, confessions of sins not committed by the person himself are often made, and there is a prayer for pardon on behalf of all Israel.

The principal holidays and festivals which come later in the Jewish year are: Sukkoth, the Festival of Booths or Tabernacles, in the month of Tishri, at the end of September or in October; Hanukkah, the Festival of Dedication, in the month of Kislev—late November or December; Hamishah Asar Bishebat, the New Year for Trees or Jewish Arbor Day, in the month of Shebat; Purim, the Feast of Lots, in the month of Adar—latter part of February or in March; Passover, the Festival of Freedom, in the month of Nisan—end of March or in April; and Shabuoth, the Festival of Weeks, in Sivan—May or early June.

There are also a number of fast days throughout the year, such as Tishah Bov, the ninth day of Ab, commemorating the destruction of the Temple in Jerusalem, and the Fast of Esther, in memory of the three days Esther fasted before asking King Ahasuerus to spare the Jews.

In contrast to the purely religious holidays—such as Yom Kippur—there are the festivals which commemorate major events in the long story of the Israelites. Foremost among these festivals are the Three Pilgrimage Feasts, which celebrate the deliverance from Egypt and the birth of the Jewish nation, about 1200 B.C. These are Passover (a literal translation of its Hebrew name, Pesach), Shabuoth, and Sukkoth. When one remembers that the Israelites were in bondage to the Egyptians for four hundred and thirty years, it is not surprising that the details of the bondage and the release, and of the wanderings at that time, are vivid in the mind of the Jewish people.

The word Passover (or Pesach) comes from the passing over or sparing of the Hebrews in Egypt when God smote the first-born of the Egyptians; but in a larger way it stands for the whole redemption from slavery. It is indeed the "Festival of Freedom." The celebration is for eight days, the first and last days being observed as holy days, when no work is done, and the intervening days being semi-holidays when one is permitted to attend to ordinary occupations.

Matzoth, or unleavened bread, is eaten during the eight days of Passover as a reminder of the long flight from Egypt when the Jews had to bake their bread as best they could without allowing time for the dough to ferment. Other foods especially made for this festival have similar meanings: for instance, the combination of nuts, apples, wine, and cinnamon known as *haroseth* looks like the brick and mortar which the people had to make when they were slaves.

A service known as the Pesach Seder is held in

Jewish homes on the first two evenings of the Passover festival. The various foods used as symbols in the service are arranged in a special dish—matsoth, bitter herbs, parsley, celery or lettuce, salt water; a combination made of nuts, apples, raisins, and wine; a roasted lamb bone, and a roasted egg. Four cups of wine called *arba kosos* are drunk by every member of the family seated around the table. And then the haggada, or narrative, which contains the ritual service and the story of Israel's exodus from Egypt, is read aloud and folk songs are sung.

A goblet of wine is always prepared for the prophet Elijah, the symbolic messenger of hope and faith. After a prayer, the door is opened so that his spirit may come in.

Shabuoth, the Festival of Weeks, the second Pilgrimage Feast, takes its name from the fact that it comes exactly seven weeks after Passover. This was originally an agricultural holiday marking the beginning of the wheat harvest. Later, when the Jews ceased to be primarily an agricultural people after the destruction of the Temple, the day served to commemorate the proclamation of the Ten Commandments at Mount Sinai. The Temple, built in Jerusalem by King Solomon in the tenth century B.C., was destroyed in 586 B.C. by King Nebuchadnezzar of Babylon when he captured Jerusalem. A new Temple on the site of the old one was built by the Jews about 537 B.C., after they returned from their captivity in Babylon.

It has been said that since tradition fixed Shabuoth as the day on which the Law was given to Israel, it is considered the religious birthday of the Jewish people, whereas Passover is considered the *national* birthday of the Jews. It has always been customary to confirm Jewish children at Shabuoth.

Sukkoth, the third Pilgrimage Feast, is the Festival of Booths or Tabernacles, reminiscent of the wanderings of the children of Israel in the wilderness after their deliverance, when they lived in little huts or "booths." During the nine days of this celebration, huts of leaves are constructed outside of the synagogue or the home, and people go into these little shelters to drink wine and eat cakes in thankfulness for the Deliverance and for the harvest time of plenty. If the hut is outside the home, all meals may be taken there. This is an autumn festival, and, like Shabuoth, was originally an agricultural celebration. It was, in fact, a kind of Thanksgiving Day.

The seventh day of Sukkoth is called Hoshanna Rabbah, "the Great Hoshanna," the eighth day is Shemini Atsereth, "the Feast of the Eighth Day," and the ninth day is Simhat Torah, "Rejoicing in the Law." The intervening days are half-holidays only. The word "Sukkoth" refers not only to the temporary dwelling places of the Jews during the Exodus, but to the impermanent dwellings of the often-persecuted Jews at all times. The feast is one of thanksgiving and joy, and in the synagogue there is singing, dancing, and general rejoicing. It is a great day for the children too, for they march around with flags, and have fruit and goodies distributed among them.

Hanukkah, the Festival of Dedication, is the week-long anniversary of the twenty-fifth of Kislev, the day on which the Temple was consecrated anew after the recapture of Jerusalem in 165 B.C. from the Syrians. It is also known as the Feast of Lights or Illumination, from a miracle which is said to have occurred during the Temple's rededication. When the perpetual lamp was about to be lighted, it was found that there was only enough oil to last one day —but by a miracle it lasted eight days, the time required for the preparation of fresh oil. In memory of this miracle, the Hanukkah lamp is kept burning on the window sill during the eight days of celebration. Little yellow wax candles or dishes of oil with threads for wicks are used: one candle is lighted for the first evening, two for the second, and so on until eight candles are burning on the eighth day. A special candle, the *shamus,* is used to light the other candles. The ceremony of lighting them is accompanied by benedictions and singing, extolling God as Israel's deliverer.

It is no wonder that this celebration is a happy one. That struggle for the regaining of Jerusalem, in which Judas Maccabaeus led a small band of Israelites to victory over a vast Syrian army, is one of the greatest events of Jewish history. To do any work by the light of Hanukkah candles is forbidden, so games are played instead. Special concerts and entertainments are held in the synagogues and Hebrew schools during the entire week. It is the custom to serve special food—*latkes,* potato pancakes, or *kugel,* a potato pie. Throughout the holiday, the children help in lighting the candles and receive presents from parents and relatives.

Purim, the Feast of Lots, is a gay time for children as well as for their elders. Presents are exchanged and in the evening every family has a party with delicious things to eat, notably the triangular cakes, filled with poppy seeds or fruit, called *haman taschen.* At one time a messenger known as the *shalach monos tregger* carried gifts from family to family, everybody went masquerading through the streets in carnival fashion, and companies of amateur actors called *Purim shpieler* (Purim Players) went from house to house dancing, singing, and giving episodes from the Purim story. Today one member of the family usually acts as *shalach monos* and carries gifts to everyone.

The Purim story, which took place in Persia in the reign of Ahasuerus, is told in the Book of Esther in the Bible. Haman, the Prime Minister, was so enraged because Mordecai, a Jew and a cousin of the beautiful Esther, refused to bow down to him that he planned to exterminate the entire Jewish people. However, Queen Esther, whose beauty and wisdom had won her the King's heart, intervened. Through her, Haman's plans were exposed. He was hanged and Mordecai was given a position of honor in the government.

There is also a Jewish Arbor Day, the observance of which has played a useful part in the rebuilding of Palestine during modern times. This is called Hamishah Asar Bishebat, or the New Year for Trees, and is observed by Jews everywhere as a spring festival. For Jews outside of Israel, it is a reminder of the homeland, and fruits which grow in Palestine are eaten: dates, figs, and pomegranates.

In the United States, "Palestinian Fruit Parties"
have long been held, and special programs are conducted in Hebrew schools and Jewish community
centers.

But the main purpose of the day is of course the
planting of trees. In ancient times, a tree was
planted for every newborn baby: a cedar for a boy,
a cypress for a girl. When it was time for the children to marry, these trees were cut down and used
as posts for the *huppah* (canopy) at the wedding
ceremony. In modern times, Hamishah Asar has
been the day for planting new trees in the Holy
Land, particularly in the Herzl Forest. Outings and
field events are held in the schools. And for years
before the new Israel became an accomplished fact,
the day was used to stimulate interest in its establishment.

No discussion of Jewish holidays is complete without mention of the Jewish Sabbath. This holiest of
all holy days falls on Saturday, the seventh day of
the week. Although the ways in which it is observed
may vary from home to home, it is always a day of
rest and prayer.

The Sabbath begins with the setting of the sun
Friday night and continues until sundown on Saturday. Friday evening the mother offers a prayer as she

lights candles in the house and then the family enjoys a special meal. After the meal, songs are sung and the father goes to the synagogue to worship.

On Saturday morning the family visits the synagogue together and afterwards returns home for the traditional lunch. The Oneg Shabbat celebration follows later in the day. Fruits and nuts are served and there are songs and stories for the children.

The Sabbath closes with the *habdala,* which means "separation." At this time the father, as head of the house, gives thanks to God for setting aside the Sabbath as a day to be distinguished from all others.

Through these Jewish holidays, so rich and fascinating in their lore and the devotion which they mirror, we may understand the history of a great people. To follow the full significance of these days through the year is to relive at first hand the colorful events and the stories that shape the lives of the people of Israel.

COLUMBUS DAY

Behind him lay the gray Azores,
　　Behind the Gates of Hercules;
Before him not the ghost of shores,
　　Before him only shoreless seas.
The good mate said: "Now must we pray,
　　For lo! the very stars are gone.
Brave Admiral, speak, what shall I say?"
　　"Why, say 'Sail on! Sail on! and on!' "

From "Columbus"
by Joaquin Miller (1841–1913)

COLUMBUS DAY, because of the unique personality of this indomitable Italian visionary who never reached Asia but did find America, is the strangely bright and different jewel in this chain of holidays. Columbus Day was first called "Discovery Day" and was set aside as a legal holiday in 1892, four hundred years after the discovery of America, by President Harrison. But how much better it is to celebrate the discoverer by name, as we do now. In all but ten states, October 12, the date Columbus made landfall in 1492, is a legal holiday. Columbus was not the first adventurer to touch land in the Western Hemisphere—others before him had come ashore.

But from his voyages came the settlement and building up of the new continent.

He was, of course, looking for Asia. Europe was greatly excited in those days by the stories Marco Polo had brought back about the wealthy East. A quicker way to this fabulous place was being sought, a passage to the west which, if the earth were round, would mean straight sailing to the Asian coast. But even Columbus did not take into account the fact that another great land mass lay between Europe and Asia.

Columbus' time was the first great age of maps. The face of the earth was a popular subject for theory and speculation. There was a period when Columbus, not yet successful in finding backers for his voyage, largely supported three families—his own, his father's, and his wife's—by drawing these maps which were so greatly in demand. His interest was shared by his wife, Felipa Moñiz, herself the daughter of a navigator who had died poor, leaving, however, an invaluable legacy of charts and instruments.

But maps cannot satisfy a born explorer for long. The time comes when he must stop tracing lines on paper and begin to follow the world's true shape on the watery globe itself. And finally, on August 3,

1492, this man of stubborn and invincible purpose did set sail with a hundred and twenty men on three ships: his own command, the *Santa Maria,* reinforced by the *Pinta,* captained by Martín Alonzo Pinzón, and the *Niña,* under Vicente Yanez Pinzón. Columbus was then about forty-six years old, if, as is thought, he was born in 1446.

It was inevitable that the adventurous and self-reliant young Columbus, born in that era and by the sea (at or near Genoa), and spending much of his early life as a sailor, should begin to think of exploring. And his indomitable character made it possible for him to persist in the long struggle to secure backing. It was not until about 1479, when he left Portugal after eight or nine years in that country and traveled to Spain with his four-year-old son Diego, that he found his first real sympathizers.

One was Fray Juan Perez de Marchena, guardian of La Rabida, the Franciscan monastery at Huelva, where Columbus and his little boy stayed for some time. The Fray had once been father confessor to Queen Isabella of Spain, and he facilitated Columbus' introduction to Isabella and Ferdinand, who finally financed the venture. On the seventeenth of April, 1492, the contract was signed by which Columbus and his heirs would forever have the title of admiral of all lands that he discovered. He was also to be viceroy and governor of such lands, and to have a tenth of the precious stones, gold, and silver found there.

The other friend, Dr. Garcia Fernandez, was a physician and student of geography in the small nearby town of Palos, the port from which Columbus sailed on his first voyage.

You probably already know the story of these four voyages, covering nine years in all. The first one ended on the island called by the Indians Guanahani and renamed San Salvador by Columbus—now generally identified with Watling's Island in the Bahamas. On a hill overlooking the bay, there is a stone shaft with the inscription:

On This Spot
Christopher Columbus
First Set Foot on the Soil of
the New World

Then he sailed along the north coast of Cuba and Haiti (Hispaniola), and built a fort on the Haitian coast called La Navidad. When he started home on January 4, 1493, he left a colony of forty men there. But when he came back to it on his second voyage late in the year, the fort was deserted; the colony had been destroyed by Indians.

This second voyage was a far more ambitious enterprise, comprising seventeen ships and fifteen hundred men. Dominica was discovered on this trip, on November 3, and in December Columbus founded Isabella, the first European town in the New World, on an island off Haiti. Then he sailed westward, discovering Jamaica. But human beings were harder to deal with than islands, and upon his return to Isabella there was much trouble with the Indians, whom he finally defeated on April 25, 1495. Then came trouble not from Indians but from Spain, where hostility had arisen against him in certain quarters. From this time on Columbus fought a double battle of exploration and of defending himself against his enemies at home.

Hostility and conspiracy of this sort can never be explained easily; usually jealousy has much to do with it. The lot of explorers has never been easy, and as Joseph Conrad, great writer and seaman, says in his essay "Geography and Some Explorers":

The greatest of them all, who has presented modern geography with a new world to work upon, was at one time loaded with chains and thrown into prison. Columbus re-

mains a pathetic figure . . . a victim of the imperfec-
tions of jealous human hearts, accepting his fate with
resignation. Among explorers he appears lofty in his
troubles and like a man of kingly nature. His contribution
to the knowledge of the earth was certainly royal.

In March, 1496, Columbus was taken back to
Spain by Juan Aguado, royal commissioner sent
out by the Spanish authorities to investigate his deal-
ings with the Indians. When Columbus presented
his case to the King, the charges were dismissed,
and he was able to start his third voyage on May
30, 1498. He discovered Trinidad in July. And the
land he found at the mouth of the Orinoco River on
August 1 was probably the first discovery of the mainland of South America.

But again an official investigator was sent, this
time Francisco de Bobadilla, and on August 24,
1500, Columbus was put into chains and returned to
Spain. Although he was released when he got there,
he was never able to regain his former honors, which
the contract had granted him for life.

On his fourth voyage, which began in March,
1502, he coasted down to the Isthmus of Panama
seeking a westward passage that would take him
home around the world, for he still believed this

land he had discovered was Asia. In February, 1503, he went back to Jamaica, and returned to Spain for the last time on November 7, 1504.

For the two years before his death on May 20 or 21, 1506, he lived in Valladolid, neglected and poverty-stricken. If Queen Isabella had not died a few weeks after he reached home, things might have been different. But the tragedy of Columbus may be overestimated. He was poor and unregarded in those last years, to be sure, but perhaps he did not die an unhappy man. It wasn't primarily gold or honors and titles that he was after, though he had hoped to have them to pass on to his sons. Most of all, he wanted the voyages, the discoveries, the sight of land, the soil under his feet, the opening up of the knowledge of the world. Columbus was a maker of maps. Because of him a new map had been made, and other, newer maps stretched away into the future. For a man who had done these things, "poor" is not the word.

Much that Columbus had lost was made up to his two sons. Diego, the elder, was created Admiral of the Indies and Governor of Hispaniola in 1509. And when Diego, like his father, had to defend himself from charges made by enemies and could not get redress for his grievances, Diego's son Luis was granted Jamaica in fief, a pension, territories in Veragua, and the titles of Duke of Veragua and Marquis of Jamaica. Luis governed Hispaniola as Captain General from 1540 to 1551, and when he in turn was banished to Oran, Africa, in 1565, the title of Duke of Veragua passed to his son, Diego, Columbus' great-grandchild, with whom the straight line of descent ended.

But it was Fernando, Columbus' second son and Diego's half-brother, who was closer to his father. Fernando had gone with his father on the fourth voyage, and he treasured the memory of this companionship more than the large royal grants he later received. He was a man of letters, building up a large library. And it was he who wrote a biography of his father. This manuscript, now lost, was used extensively by Bartolomé de Las Casas, a Dominican missionary and historian, whose work has been a valuable source of information on Columbus to scholars for many years.

HALLOWEEN

Amang the bonnie winding banks,
   Where Doon rins, wimpling clear,
Where Bruce ance rul'd the martial ranks,
   And shook his Carrick spear,
Some merry, friendly, countra folks,
   Together did convene,
To burn the nits, an' pou their stock,
   An' haud their Halloween
            Fu' blythe that night.

From "Halloween"
by Robert Burns (1759–1796)

HALLOWEEN, IN spite of the fact that it takes its name from a Christian festival (All Hallows or All Saints' Day), comes from pagan times and has never taken on a Christian significance.

There were two different festivals in the early world at this time of year, and they are both represented in our own Halloween activities. When you duck for apples, or throw an apple paring over your shoulder to see what initial it makes on the floor, you are doing as the Romans did—honoring Pomona, the Roman goddess of orchards and especially of apple orchards. And when you light a candle inside the jeering pumpkin face, you are in a small way imitating the Celtic Druids of northern Britain (described in the chapter on Saint Patrick's Day), who lit a fire to scare away winter and the evil spirits who were waiting to come rushing in when summer was over.

On that night between October and November, the Druids kindled great fires on the hills as a barrier against the evil to come. (These Halloween fires still burn every year in many places, but especially in Scotland and Wales.) By waving burning wisps of plaited straw aloft on pitchforks, people tried to frighten off demons and witches, but just in case this didn't work, they also put on grotesque and terrifying costumes. For if you dressed in a horrible enough fashion and went trooping around with the spirits all night, they would think you were one of them, and do you no harm. This is where the persistent Halloween custom of "dressing up" and wearing masks originated; and among the children who come to the door on Halloween, calling "trick or treat," the most alarming costumes are still considered the best.

Other northern peoples in the Germanic and Scandinavian countries also lived in terror of "the raging rout," as they called the evil spirits whom they believed to be led by the great god Odin. Halloween weather was of the greatest importance to these people, for the day was prophetic: if the rout came in on a soft wind, the next year would be easy and good; but if the rout came raging in, the year would be full of bitter woe and warfare.

The night being so filled with supernatural powers, it was usually possible for individuals to catch some premonitions of their own futures. Especially among the Celts there was a custom—which still continues —to try to learn what the future holds, especially in matrimonial matters. There is a wistful line in an old Scotch song, "But I don't know whom I'll marry." Well, Halloween is the time to find out. And if you can't get some kind of a hint at least, you must have no Celtic blood at all. There are so many ways that there should be one for everybody.

For instance, a girl puts three nuts on the grate. Then she names one nut for herself, and two for possible husbands of her acquaintance. He who cracks or jumps will be unfaithful, but he who starts to burn really likes her and will be a good mate. If the girl's nut and one of the others burn together, then the wedding is certain. Also, there is an interesting method of looking into a mirror. But, of course, a girl must be eating an apple while doing it. Then, if she "gets a sight"—sees a boy peeping over her shoulder—the boy she sees will be the one she will marry.

There are also the Three Luggies, or dishes, which Robert Burns mentions in his poem, "Halloween." This is for boys instead of girls. One dish holds clean water, one dirty water, and one is empty. The boy is blindfolded, and dips his fingers into the first dish he feels. Clean water, as you can guess, means he will wed a maiden, dirty water a widow, and if the dish is empty, he stays single. Boys being never so eager to marry as girls are, the empty dish is probably a great relief to them.

Nuts and apples are the invariable attendants upon all Halloween feasts, both then and now. In fact, in the north of England Halloween is often called "Nutcrack Night." And in Penzance and St. Ives, in Cornwall, the Saturday nearest Halloween is known as "Allan Day," after the big red apples of the region—apples from ancient orchards which have supplied many generations of Halloween believers.

"Trick or treat" means of course that the young Halloween visitors who come to your door will play no tricks on you if you will "treat" them—ask them in for cookies or cider, maybe, and help fill their bags with fruit, nuts, cake, candy, or anything else you think they might like. But in the earlier days of our American Halloweens, before "tricks or treats" became popular, the night of October 31 was a nervous time for houseowners. People who had such things as birdbaths, gates, and lawn chairs learned to stow them away somewhere before dusk arrived and the "raging rout" of children, dressed as demons, ghosts, and witches started to lug away and hide every movable thing they could find.

That mischief making is almost entirely over and the "evil spirits" are turned into just a lot of friendly neighborhood children by the ancient Halloween magic of apples, nuts, and general merriment. We wish the Druids and the Romans and the Norse could have found as simple a way out.

ELECTION DAY

As noiseless fall those printed slips
　　As fall the silent dews of night,
Yet never words from human lips
　　Had greater majesty and might.

Administrations rise and fall,
　　And parties rise or cease to be,
Obedient to the ballot's call,
　　The weapon of a people free.

From "The Ballot"
by William G. Haeselbarth

THE POEM on the opposite page was written in the old days before voting machines, when voters marked a long piece of paper and dropped it into a ballot box. Ballot boxes are becoming obsolete, but the words the poet uses to describe the ballot remain true—it is "The weapon of a people free." When you pull down those little levers on the voting machine, you have played an important part in the operation of a free society.

Election Day is different from other holidays; it isn't just for pleasure, or for remembering and honoring some person or event. It is a day strictly in the present and for the future, a day when you have a duty to perform. The fact that voting is also one of your greatest privileges makes it even more a duty. Nothing you do through the rest of the year is of greater importance. Nor is being a voter just the work of that minute behind the voting-machine curtain. To decide exactly what your wishes are has already taken thought, information, and judgment. To vote is a good thing in itself; but to have good reasons for the way you vote is a better thing. And, as you very well know, family tradition or other prejudices are not good reasons. If you're old enough to vote, you're old enough to have convictions of your own. Fine, if your grandfather and you do happen to agree—but not if you agree only because he is your grandfather. Nor, on the other hand, is it of any value to deviate from family practice simply because of defiance and the desire to be different.

The ideal of democracy is an old one. Ancient Greece was probably the first country to achieve it, and in ancient Greece the first ballots were cast. Balls, stones, shells, or potsherds (pieces of broken earthen pots) were marked and used for the purpose. (The word "ballot" comes to us directly from the French *ballotte*, ball.) In Rome, the ballots were *tabulae*, or tickets.

Our country became the first modern republic after the American Revolution. France also became a republic after her revolution of 1789. There is no need to tell you of the widespread democratization of European countries in the years between and since the two World Wars.

Our own plan of government—which is the basis of our voting—was determined by our Constitution, drawn up by a special convention at Philadelphia in 1787. This provided the system by which our affairs are administered under three heads: the legislative, or law-making, department, consisting of the Senate and House of Representatives; the executive, or law-executing, department, consisting of the President, the Vice-President, and other civil officers; and the judicial, or law-interpreting, department, consisting of the various courts headed by the Supreme Court. Some of these many officers are appointed; others are elected.

Election Day was established as the Tuesday after the first Monday in November by act of Congress on January 23, 1845. It is a legal holiday in five states: New Jersey, New York, Ohio, Pennsylvania, and Virginia. The presidential election, every four years, is naturally the most exciting one, but that day without the Election Days in between would be like a flower minus root or stem—it wouldn't exist. So every "first Tuesday after the first Monday in November," that variable but urgent date, is just as necessary as every other. United States Senators are elected every six years. Congressional Representatives are elected every two years. State governors have terms of different lengths. And besides these, the other state officers, and the innumerable local officeholders of the counties and towns, must be chosen on Election Day, though special elections are sometimes held for local candidates.

Some holidays perhaps lose a little of their magic as we grow older. Not so Election Day, a holiday which never ceases to grow in interest and importance as we become more personally involved in its outcome. Each year it has a new and unique significance.

VETERANS' DAY
(formerly Armistice Day)

The fighting man shall from the sun
  Take warmth, and life from the glowing earth;
Speed with the light-foot winds to run,
  And with the trees to newer birth;
And find, when fighting shall be done,
  Great rest, and fullness after dearth.

From "Into Battle"
by Julian Grenfell (1888–1915)

WHEN PEOPLE woke up on the morning of November 11, 1918, they didn't know it was a holiday. It wasn't a holiday, in fact, until nearly noon, when the news was flashed to every corner of our country that at eleven o'clock Eastern Standard Time the Armistice had been signed, and the First World War was over. At that moment the holiday began, with terrific speed and all-out rejoicing. It had seemed that the day would never come—but now it had come at last, and all of a sudden. Every town and tiny village found its own ways to celebrate. The cities went wild. Workers rushed out of office buildings in a body. Groups of strangers found themselves bound together by streamers of confetti and paper

—to show that on that day nobody was a stranger. The streets were filled from curb to curb with marching, shouting, embracing, laughing, crying people. And the churches were full of people thanking God.

That was the first, the original Armistice Day. In 1921 it was made a legal holiday by Congress. And so dear was this day to people in every part of the country that it took its place as one of the seven legal holidays observed by all states.

But then we had to fight in other foreign wars, and the name Armistice Day, applying to the First World War only, was no longer adequate. In June, 1954, President Eisenhower signed a bill making it Veterans' Day, and now in the ranks on ranks of men marching in the November 11 parades there are more veterans from the Korean War and from the Second World War than from the First.

This was our first and only holiday to spring up from global conflict and the military entrance of the United States into world affairs. After two more wars, it is hard for us today to imagine the consternation Americans felt the first time we were forced to enter a widespread war in Europe.

The United States tried hard to keep out of the conflict. President Woodrow Wilson had been chosen by the people for a second term in office because he believed in neutrality. But as the war went on, Germany sank or threatened so many of our ships that we were compelled to take sides against her. On an April day in 1917, after the war had been going on for almost three years, Congress formally declared war on Germany, and preparations went forward with the greatest possible haste to get an army ready for service abroad.

When the first detachment of troops passed through London, they made quite a stir; this was something entirely new. But within the next few months our troops poured into France in ever-increasing numbers, and soon they were taken as a matter of course. Early in the final year of the war, 1918, America had a million soldiers in active service, and another million in training.

In a car in a railway train in the Forest of Compiègne, France, where Marshal Ferdinand Foch, commander in chief of the Allied armies, had his headquarters, the German delegates were received and the Armistice was signed at five o'clock in the morning (their time) on November 11, 1918. It was hoped that this war would be the war to end all wars; sadly, it was not. Is it too much to hope that someday early in the morning (their time or ours) some final Armistice will be negotiated, and the world will remain at peace?

THANKSGIVING

Season of mists and mellow fruitfulness!
Close bosom-friend of the maturing sun;
Conspiring with him how to load and bless
With fruit the vines that round the thatch-eaves run;
To bend with apples the mossed cottage-trees,
And fill all fruit with ripeness to the core;
To swell the gourd, and plump the hazel shells
With a sweet kernel; to set budding more,
And still more, later flowers for the bees,
Until they think warm days will never cease,
For Summer has o'erbrimmed their clammy cells.

From "To Autumn"
by John Keats (1795–1821)

Our harvest being gotten in," Edward Winslow of the Plymouth Colony wrote in December, 1621, to a friend in England, "our governor sent four men on fowling, that so we might after a special manner, rejoice together after we had gathered the fruit of our labors." So into the new country came the world-old practice of putting the harvest to a festive use; and thus began our great autumn holiday of feasting and of thankfulness.

That was a magnificent festival, in 1621. "Dinner" would hardly be the word. The Indian guests, for one thing, had no idea of returning home that night, and the feasting went on. And then after three days, just so there would be no danger of running out of food, the Indians went out and shot five more deer. The Indian chief Massasoit had ninety of his men around the table, which must have been a very long one.

"And although it is not always so plentiful as it was at this time with us," concluded Winslow (who, incidentally, later became governor of Plymouth Colony himself), "yet by the goodness of God, we are so far from want, that we wish you partakers of our plenty." Which sums up the spirit of Thanksgiving, then, now, and always.

Harvests were gathered every year, and thanks were given, but Thanksgiving Day did not become nationally celebrated until 242 years later, during the presidency of Abraham Lincoln. In 1789 President Washington, at the request of Congress, had proclaimed November 26 for the purpose, but the day was observed in the Northern states only. Only in 1864, when Lincoln set aside the last Thursday in November, did Thanksgiving Day become an established holiday. So much an established holiday, in fact, that in 1939 when President Franklin D. Roosevelt changed the day from the fourth to the third Thursday of the month, there was nation-wide consternation, and by 1941 Thanksgiving was back where it always had been.

It is the most natural thing in the world for people to laugh and sing when they have their barns filled and when their work in the hot summer sun is over—when the harvest is home. No words could describe the reason for a holiday of thanksgiving more accurately than the words of the old English song "Harvest Home." The jubilant people sang the simplest kind of song—but it tells the story.

> *Harvest home! harvest home!*
> *We've ploughed, we've sowed,*
> *We've reaped, we've mowed,*
> *We've brought home every load.*
> *Hip, hip, hip, harvest home!*

No wonder they dressed themselves up in grain sheaves, had fantastic parades in honor of the last wagon in from the fields, and contended in all kinds of rustic sports—much as had the Romans before them when *their* barns were full. Indeed, as far back as history reaches, "harvest home" has called for merrymaking and for honoring the gods who foster crops. In Rome the goddess was Ceres and her day, October 4, was the "Cerelia" (which shows us where our word, *cereal*, originated). In ancient Greece the goddess was Demeter, responsible for the soil and all that grew therein. Athens was wonderfully gay on those three days in November when Demeter was presented with a cow and a sow, as well as honey, poppies, corn, and fruit. The Canaanites, in the Book of Judges in the Bible, "went out in the field, and gathered their vineyards, and trod the grapes and held festival, and went into the house of their God, and did eat and drink." And in the Middle Ages there was the Feast of St. Martin of Tours, on November 11, now Martinmas.

Roast goose was the thing to eat on St. Martin's Day—"Martin's goose," they called it. And nothing must be drunk but "Saint Martin's wine," the first wine made from the grapes of the recent harvest. Goose remained for a long time the traditional thanksgiving fare. Those Pilgrims who planned the feast back in 1621 probably expected that the four men who went hunting would just naturally bring in more wild geese than anything else. But as it happened, wild geese were not so very plentiful in the New World. Turkey seemed to predominate. And, up to this year of thankfulness, they still do.

For what would Thanksgiving be without turkey and the fixin's—the gravy and the dressing (oyster dressing, chestnut dressing, or whatever is the favorite with your family); mashed potatoes, sweet potatoes, turnips, creamed onions, and every other vegetable you can think of; celery and olives, both the ripe ones and the stuffed; not to mention mince pies, pumpkin pies, and a dozen other things!

Fortunately we have no three-day Indian guests nowadays, but only families and friends who fill a table reasonably sized and feel well satisfied with just one meal. For what a meal it is!

CHRISTMAS

A CHRISTMAS CAROL

I heard the bells on Christmas Day
Their old, familiar carols play,
    And wild and sweet
    The words repeat
Of peace on earth, good-will to men!

And thought how, as the day had come,
The belfries of all Christendom
    Had rolled along
    The unbroken song
Of peace on earth, good-will to men!

Till, ringing, singing on its way,
The world revolved from night to day,
    A voice, a chime,
    A chant sublime,
Of peace on earth, good-will to men! . . .

From "Christmas Bells"
by Henry Wadsworth Longfellow (1807–1882)

PROBABLY ANY one of us could write this chapter about the last, best holiday of the year. No two descriptions would be the same, for our memories and associations are our own. But for every Christian, and for many non-Christians in countries where Christian customs are well known, this great combined holyday and holiday is touched with special magic. The great feast of the Christ child's birth has become the feast of all children, and of all love and friendship, set off from other days as a carol is from other songs.

A great census of the world was being taken, in that year which began the Christian era. And Joseph, because he was of the house of David, went with Mary his wife to register in the town of David called Bethlehem. While they were there, Mary "brought forth her first-born son, and wrapped him in swaddling clothes, and laid him in a manger; because there was no room for them in the inn." We all know the beautiful story of how the shepherds came to see the Child, guided by a star, and how twelve days later (now Twelfth Night or Epiphany) the Wise Men from the East reached the end of their journey, bringing Him gifts of frankincense and myrrh. Twelfth Night is for that reason considered the real end of the Christmas season, when decorations are taken down and, much as we hate to part with it, the Christmas tree must go. As Robert Herrick wrote, in the seventeenth century:

> *Down with the Rosemary, and so*
> *Down with the Baies and mistletoe;*
> *Down with the Holly, Ivie, all*
> *Wherewith ye drest the Christmas Hall.*

No matter how long we make it last, this is a holiday which never outwears its welcome.

It is of course true, that the birth of Christ began the Christian era. But we now know that Christ was not born in the year One of our calendar. The Apostles did not record the year of His birth, and when the scholarly monk Dionysius Exiquus worked out the first Christian calendar in the sixth century, the date was miscalculated by at least four years. Later scholars have determined that Christ's birthday must have been between 7 B.C. and 4 B.C., but it has not been thought necessary to change the calendar to correct the error. Christmas is Christmas, no matter when it began.

Nor are the exact month and day known. The date of December twenty-fifth was established about the year 320, largely in order to unify it with the Saturnalia, the pagan feast celebrating the winter solstice, which came on that day. Since about A.D. 400 this date has been kept by the whole Christian Church —although the December 25 of the Greek churches, which follow the old Julian calendar, falls on January 7 of our calendar.

The legends about this magical season are very beautiful. As Shakespeare says in *Hamlet:*

Some say that ever 'gainst that season comes
Wherein our Saviour's birth is celebrated,
The bird of dawning singeth all night long:
And then, they say, no spirit dare stir abroad;
The nights are wholesome, then no planets strike,
No fairy takes, nor witch hath power to charm,
So hallowed and so gracious is the time.

Festivities include customs from the pre-Christian world, not only from the Roman winter festival, but also from the northern merrymaking called Yule, which honored the god Thor. An old song sung in England says:

> *Come, bring with a noise,*
> *My merrie, merrie boyes,*
> *The Christmas log to the firing.*

It is the Yule log it refers to, and those first original "boyes" were Saxons, eager as we are for a proper celebration of their holiday.

Carols are the very voice of Christmas. We hear them at church, at home, from loudspeakers in the streets and stations, on radio and TV, everywhere; and without them the day would be mute and incomplete. These delicate and fanciful songs for the Christ child have come down to us from many countries. "Carol" in medieval England meant dancing in a ring while singing; and, before that, flute music also went with the dancing and the singing, for as Francis X. Weiser tells us in *The Christmas Book,* the word "carol" comes from the Greek word *choraulein,* which is made up of two others—*choros,* the dance, and *aulein,* to play the flute.

There is delight and tenderness in carols, pick

them where we may. Here is a Spanish carol called in English, "What Shall I Give to the Child in the Manger?"

What shall I give to the Child in the Manger?
What shall I give to the beautiful Boy?
Grapes I will give to Him, hanging in clusters,
Baskets of figs for the Child to enjoy.
  Tam-pa-tan-tam, when the figs will have ripened,
  Tam-pa-tan-tam, they will add to His joy!

What shall I give to the Child in the manger?
What shall I give to the beautiful Boy?
Garlands of flowers to twine in His fingers,
Cherries so big for the Child to enjoy.
  Tam-pa-tan-tam, when the cherries have ripened,
  Tam-pa-tan-tam, they will add to His joy!

From France comes a great favorite, "Un Flambeau, Jeannette, Isabelle," which we call, "Bring a Torch, Jeannette, Isabella":

  Bring a torch, Jeannette, Isabella,
  Bring a torch, and quickly run,
  Christ is born, good folk of the village,
  Christ is born, and Mary's calling,
    Ah! ah! beautiful is the Mother,
    Ah! ah! beautiful is Her Son.

Quiet all, nor waken Jesus,
Quiet all, and whisper low,
Silence all, and gather around Him,
Talk and noise might waken Jesus.
  Hush! hush! quietly now He slumbers,
  Hush! hush! quietly now He sleeps.

The earliest English carol known to us dating from the beginning of the fifteenth century, is, as are so many carols, a lullaby:

I saw a sweet, a seemly sight,
A blissful bird, a blossom bright,
That mourning made and mirth among:
A maiden mother meek and mild
In cradle keep a knave child
That softly slept; she sat and sung:
  Lullay, lulla, balow,
  My bairn, sleep softly now.

(The word "knave" then meant simply "boy." It is closely akin to the German word for boy, *Knabe.*)

The widespread custom of giving Christmas presents goes back, without a doubt, to those first hours of the Christ child's life. The first Christmas presents were for Him. History does not tell of any gifts until the Wise Men, twelve days later, brought their gold and frankincense and myrrh—but surely the other people who were around Him from the first found something they could give Him. "What shall I give to the Child in the manger?" (as the carol says) must have been the thought in everybody's heart. The shepherds, says a Belgian carol, brought milk and cheese and cake.

The Child not only received presents but He also gave them. For in early Christian tradition, although St. Nicholas, patron of children, brought gifts on the eve of December sixth, the Christ child Himself brought them on Christmas Eve. The two traditions of gift-giving are combined in Santa Claus. No longer holy though so much beloved, he has made a long journey down through Christian folklore. The name "St. Nicholas" was finally pronounced in Holland "Sinter Klaas," and from this it is thought that our "Santa Claus" finally emerged, when in the seventeenth century the Dutch brought their Christmas celebrations with them to New Amsterdam (later New York). Now the whole Christian world, grown-up as well as youthful, gives and receives presents; and although they are no longer to or from the Child, they are still because of Him.

The first presents given at this time of year, at the Roman Saturnalia which began on December 17, were green branches for good luck. Way back in the reign of King Tatius of the Sabines, the King received this woodland token from a "lucky tree" in the grove of Strenae. The branches (and later fruits, cakes, and other things as well) were therefore called *strenae*. Since the Saturnalia was celebrated up through the Calends (or first) of January, the branches were also one of the earliest ways of wishing Happy New Year. Green, in those days of nature worship, was for luck and for warding off evil. And even now, for the Christian festival, to "bring home Christmas" is to bring into the house the beauty and the blessing of the woods and outdoor world. What would Christmas be for any of us without the green—the holly and the mistletoe, the evergreen boughs and, above all, the tree?

One of the most magical things about the night when Christ was born was that all the trees in the forests bloomed and bore fruit. This legend appeared in many forms and in many lands. And our Christmas tree, it is often said, is an incarnation of that lovely and long-held belief. To decorate a midwinter tree as we do is to bring legendry to life. And now that so many living outdoor trees are also being hung with light and color, we are coming even closer to that original idea.

Of course trees by their very nature invite decoration—certain trees more than others. A fine book, *Christmas Tradition,* by William Muir Auld, tells us that the Arabians long ago spoke of their date palm as "a tree to hang things on." Virgil told how the Romans "hang soft masks from the tall pine" for the god Bacchus. We all know of instances of decorating trees; for example, the Maypole with its ribbons and garlands. Trees have always been very close to men, an integral part of their worship and their play.

The Christmas tree itself, however, does not go far back into early tradition, as do our other Christmas greens. The custom of dressing a tree to symbolize the wonder and joy of Christmas began in late sixteenth- or early seventeenth-century Germany, after the Reformation, the movement to reform the Church in which Martin Luther, a German, was the first great leader. One story says that Luther himself had the first inspiration for the tree when he came back from a Christmas Eve walk and, to suggest the beauty of the night sky, set up for his children a candle-lighted tree. This may very well be true, even though it was fifty years after Luther's death that the first written mention of a Christmas tree was made. An unknown travel-book writer, around 1604, tells how "At Christmas they set up fir trees in the parlors at Strasburg and hang thereon roses cut out of many-colored paper, apples, wafers, gold-foil, sweets, etc."

The custom grew and flourished in Germany, but it was not until the nineteenth century that it spread very generally to the other Christian countries. Paris had its first Christmas tree in 1840, and Queen Victoria introduced it into Windsor Castle in 1841, the second year of her marriage, when her first child, later Edward VII, was a baby. After that, it didn't take long for the tree to cross the Atlantic and reach us.

We all know how the tree has become more and more the center of Christmas celebration, civic as well as home. No longer does "Christmas tree" mean just the fragrance which it spreads about it in our homes, or the sight of the well-loved ornaments which we have known from childhood. Now it often means also the trees which live with us on lawn or in garden, becoming festive strangers once a year. In many towns and villages it means the community tree. And in large cities it means the giants which are brought from forests by almost unimaginable means, to tower over square or park or plaza. When their multitudinous lights suddenly break forth on Christmas Eve, the transformation is almost as miraculous in its electrical way as when, in that first recognition of the day, all the trees of the winter woods burst into bloom.

HOLIDAYS OF
OTHER COUNTRIES

THE BRITISH ISLES

The holidays we remember best from childhood
are those in which there was some special kind of
colorful celebration—when, in fact, we had the most
fun. When an Englishman who has lived in this
country for a long time heard that we were writing
about English holidays, he at once began to recall
his own favorites. Empire Day (now called Commonwealth Day) was the one that came to his mind
first. They used to dress up, he said, in the costumes
of the colonies in the far-flung parts of the British
Empire, now the British Commonwealth of Nations.
They preferred, of course, the farthest-off and

strangest parts: Zanzibar, Malaya, Somaliland, and the others. He had forgotten the date and had never even known that it was Queen Victoria's birthday which was, and still is, celebrated on the twenty-fourth of May.

Although Victoria's birthday continues to be celebrated, the birthday of the reigning sovereign is always a holiday too. Every year the official birthday —distinct from the actual birthday—of Queen Elizabeth II is celebrated in early June, as was that of her father, King George VI. It is one of the pictures of her that we enjoy most: on horseback, reviewing her troops, with a fine white plume in her hat.

Twelfth Night, the evening of Twelfth Day or Epiphany, is a centuries-old night of merrymaking in England; Shakespeare's play, *Twelfth Night*, was especially written to be acted on this holiday. On Candlemas Day, the Festival of the Virgin on February second, candles are blessed and placed on the altars. In Scotland the day is important for prophesying the weather:

> *If Candlemas Day be dry and fair,*
> *The half o' winter's come and mair;*
> *If Candlemas Day be wet and foul,*
> *The half o' winter was gone at Youl.*

Customs have a curious way of passing from country to country, and in the United States Candlemas Day has become our Groundhog Day, when we prophesy weather according to whether the little creature can see his own shadow when he comes out to look around. If it's sunny and he *can* see it, he runs back into his burrow for six more weeks of winter. This is the only case we know of where sunshine is a bad omen.

Shrove Tuesday, the day before Lent, is called "Pancake Day" in England. As in other lands, where it is known as Mardi Gras or Fat Tuesday, this is the last chance for carnival and feasting before the forty-day fast begins. All kinds of games were played in the old days, and prominent among the good things to eat were pancakes. "Throwing the pancake" was the phrase for the fun: the same flipping motion which makes us call pancakes "flapjacks" in this country. *Poor Robin's Almanac* for the year 1684 tells how at the solemn summons of a bell in the church tower, all workers laid down their tools, saying to themselves,

> *But hark! I hear the pancake bell,*
> *And fritters make a gallant smell.*

The traditional game of throwing the pancake is still observed in some of the prep schools of England, where with great ceremony a pancake is tossed over the boundary which separates upper and lower classmen. Then follows a fight for possession of the pancake.

English Easter customs are much the same as in our own and other countries, centering largely around eggs, rabbits, and other tokens of spring. But the old "lifting" tradition belongs to England only. This is said to have originated in the thirteenth century, in the time of King Edward I. That monarch gave presents of money to those of his retainers who first called upon him on Easter morning and lifted him from his bed, in memory of Christ's rising from the sepulcher. In some country districts older members of the family are still "lifted," and presents are given.

May Day, a holiday inherited from the Romans, has always been one of the merriest days of the English year, as we know from our chapter, "May Day." There is still no village complete without its Maypole on the first of May, and in some places in both England and Ireland horses are sometimes persuaded to wear garlands and jingle-jangle bells. The old saying, "There will always be an England," might almost read, "There will always be a May Day," and would give much the same meaning of tradition and love of country life.

Another important day in the British Isles is Guy Fawkes' Day. The old rhyme which bids the people

Please to remember
The fifth of November

has never really been needed, for there is always a fascination about bonfires, especially when effigies are to be burned on them. These bonfires are in memory of the failure of the "Gunpowder Plot" to burn up King and Parliament back in the reign of James I. Guy Fawkes, the ringleader of the conspiracy, was actually about to touch off some barrels of gunpowder under the House of Lords, when he was seized and hustled off to judgment. His execution, in 1606, is still commemorated in many places by this burning of his "effigy," the unfortunate dummy constructed only to be destroyed.

The English Christmas, to which our own Christmas owes so much, with its boar's head, its wassail bowl, and its cakes—and especially the plum pudding, brandy lighted and burning blue—makes the old Italian proverb very apt when it says of a busy man, "He has more to do than the ovens of England at Christmas."

English boys are very busy people. They are not only bonfire fans and masqueraders, but also choirboys. As long as their soprano voices hold out, they take active vocal parts in the Church of England holidays. They not only cherish the joyful services of Christmas, Easter, and the other red-letter days, but also the gala times that follow these holidays: Boxing Day, Easter Monday, and Whitmonday. Boxing Day, the first weekday after Christmas, is not, as might be supposed, a signal for putting on the gloves, but rather the charitable and friendly time when Christmas boxes are distributed to postmen, errand boys, and employees in general. Whitmonday is the day following Whitsunday (the seventh Sunday after Easter). These days are called bank holidays, a term meaning any holiday on which the banks are closed.

The "red–letter days," Church of England holidays, take their name from the fact that they are printed in red on the calendar. They include Epiphany, or Twelfth Day, on January 6; Candlemas Day, on the second of February; Shrove Tuesday, the day before Lent begins; All Saints' Day, on the first of November, and others.

In Ireland, of course, Saint Patrick's Day is the greatest holiday and holyday, on the much-loved seventeenth of March, the day the great saint died. In Scotland the patron saint is Saint Andrew who, among other things, is believed to have initiated the great national game of golf—and no greater compliment could be paid him than that, for the Scots love golf. His birthday is the thirtieth of November, and is celebrated with fairs and banquets and more lightheartedness than the Scot is usually given credit for. Nor is Saint Andrew indifferent to romance, for Saint Andrew's Eve is the traditional time for the young people to exchange vows and what were called in older days "love charms." New Year's Day, as we have already seen, is also a great holiday of the Scottish people. The New Year's Eve song, *Auld Lang Syne,* sung sadly and proudly at the stroke of twelve by English-speaking people in all parts of the world, hails from Scotland's own poet, Robbie Burns:

> *Should auld acquaintance be forgot,*
> *And never brought to mind?*
> *Should auld acquaintance be forgot,*
> *And days o' auld lang syne?*

Wales is the great country for music, especially singing, and the Eisteddfod is their famous festival. Since the days of the chieftains, the best singers and players have been rewarded for their performances during that great music match. Each year the first week in August is given over to this magnificent contest of poetry and song, when harpers and singers from every town come together to test their prowess in these arts. There is a great deal of ceremony connected with this week, which begins with the blowing of trumpets "to the four corners of the world." And in no corner of the world is music, or any other art, better served than here.

FRANCE

A country's most interesting holidays are the ones most distinctively its own. In France there are three we think of at once, belonging to France alone: two very serious historical dates, Bastille Day, July 14, and Joan of Arc's Day, on the second Sunday of May; and the more lightly celebrated Saint Catherine's Day on the twenty-fifth of November.

Bastille Day is the national independence day of the French, as the Fourth of July is ours; it dates from their important year of 1789 as ours dates from 1776. The Bastille, a huge jail-fortress which stood in the heart of Paris, had become a symbol of tyranny and oppression. With its fall, on July 14, 1789, at the peak of the French Revolution, independence and republican government came to the French people—for the freeing of the prison inmates meant the much larger freedom of the nation. A monument now marks the place where that dreaded building stood, and all over France, and especially in Paris, the anniversary is hailed with joy. On the evening before, a torchlight parade begins the jubilation. At daybreak a hundred cannon shots are fired, and Bastille Day goes forward with games, fireworks, and dancing in the streets.

The day which honors Joan of Arc, the Maid of Orléans (Saint Jeanne since she was canonized by the Roman Catholic Church in 1920), is a more solemn one. It is celebrated on Sunday and there is no dancing; but in all of France—especially the towns of Orléans and Rouen, where her victory and her martyrdom took place—the streets are decorated with streamers and with pictures and statues of the adored "Maid." The history of her life you know: how her visions led her to the defense of France when part of the country was conspiring with England and had actually put an English king on the French throne in place of the rightful Charles VII. On April 29, 1429, leading the troops which raised the siege of Orléans, she saved France for the French king and people. Her trial was in Rouen, where she was burned at the stake.

On Saint Catherine's Day, November 25, comes a celebration of a very different kind. This is the parade of the *midinettes,* or sewing girls—a playful kind of ceremony which seems to us so typically French. To "put on Saint Catherine's cap" means that a girl is in danger of becoming a spinster; so it is only those over twenty-five who do the parading, dressing up in white caps and aprons and paying gay tribute to Saint Catherine, the patroness of old maids. This is a day given over to jokes and laughter, and designed to ease the heart of any young woman who is getting really worried.

France is primarily a Roman Catholic country and the Church holidays are observed in much the same way as in other countries, though with a few local variations. Some rural parts of France still celebrate the eve of Saint Nicholas, December 6, when the saint used to come bringing presents to the children. Christmas Eve has always been a time especially for the singing of carols and worship at the *crèche,* or cradle. *Noël,* which means both Christmas and Christmas carol, is a beloved word in France, and a beautiful one.

In Provence and other southern districts, children set out on the eve of Epiphany, January 6, with gifts of fruit and cake for the Christ child, hoping that on their way they will meet the Wise Men, who will deliver the gifts for them. If they do not meet the Magi, they lay their offerings on the altar of the church instead.

Easter Monday, as in England and several other European countries, is a holiday, and so is Whitmonday, the day after Whitsunday, seventh Sunday after Easter. At the Easter High Mass, candles are blessed for family use. As these must last the whole year, they are lighted only for solemn occasions such as weddings and funerals.

The South of France particularly loves Mardi Gras, the carnival which ushers in Lent. In Nice the processions are outstandingly elaborate and grotesque, with King Carnival and his court of imps, floats of flowers put to imaginative uses, and a real-life "Fat Ox" garlanded with streamers, a tantalizing reminder that this is the last meat-eating day for a while.

On Corpus Christi, the festival in honor of the Blessed Sacrament, which usually comes in early June, the whole countryside is turned into a church. The bread and wine are taken from the church altars and in dishes of silver and gold they are carried through the streets, past houses bedecked in their honor. France is not alone in this Corpus Christi custom of taking the church out into the world of nature; other southern countries do the same. But each countryside is different, and when the small altars, covered with boughs and flowers, are set up at every crossroads, this is France at its loveliest and most devout.

In Brittany since very early times there has been a festival in honor of Saint Anne, mother of the Virgin Mary. This falls on July 25 and lasts for two days, so that time be given for the people to make pilgrimage to the shrine of the saint.

Along with the other countries we have spoken of in our chapter, "Halloween," France has inherited the witchery of that night when witches and demons used to come roaring into the world to play havoc. Anyone venturing through a French graveyard on the eve of All Saints' Day, November 1, may hear bones rattling from behind gravestones, and see skulls grinning suddenly from the dark, their eye sockets horribly alight. Whether these are real skulls or just make-believe ones like our pumpkins, we are not sure. Probably, since the supply of available skulls is never large, they are only pumpkins or something else easily scooped out to make the likeness of a skeleton face. Anyway, the French children seem to have a strong streak of realism, sticking close to the graveyard for their gruesome fun.

France's newest legal holiday is May 8, that unforgettable day when the Second World War came to an end in Europe. This now overshadows the first Armistice Day, November 11—a date which since 1918 has been celebrated at the Arc de Triomphe, where the body of France's Unknown Soldier lies buried. Both days, though belonging not to France alone, are proud additions to the list of French holidays.

GERMANY

Germany in the old days—both as the German Empire and, after the First World War, as the Republic of Germany—was famous for the warmhearted *Gemütlichkeit,* or homelike quality, of its holydays and festivals. Then came the Nazi (National Socialist) regime under Adolf Hitler, 1933–1945. Church holidays fell out of favor, and under this rule, so unsympathetic to most of the people, there was little heart for the other celebrations, with their familiar customs, family sentiment, and carefree recreation. The old Germany was in eclipse.

The Second World War ended this regime, and Hitler, foreseeing the total defeat of his "Third Reich," killed himself. But in the years since 1945 Germany has remained unsettled. The history of these years is of course familiar to us all. The country was divided into zones under the governing authority of the various allies. But after three years of conflict between England, France, and the United States on the one hand, and Russia on the other, Germany was partitioned into two distinct areas under rival political and economic rule: West Germany, under England, France, and the United States, took the name of the Federal Republic of Germany; and East Germany, under Russia, became the German Democratic Republic. How the German people themselves feel about this matter is made clear by the number of refugees who have come from the East to the West since 1945: one estimate is that in the first dozen years there have been well over thirteen million.

A violent expression of the people's feeling burst forth in a riot of workers on June 17, 1953, and this day has become a new holiday: the Day of German Unity. The June 17 riot broke out in the Russian sector of Berlin, becoming a revolution which spread rapidly all over East Germany. Certain limited compromises in workers' living conditions were made by the Communist rulers as a result of the outbreak. And it also served as an example for the later revolution in Hungary. June 17 was proclaimed a holiday by the Parliament of the Federal Republic, or West Germany, and it has become a day of great importance to the German people.

In the Federal Republic, of course, there are no restrictions of any kind on the old holidays, and among these holidays the church festivals rank high. They are celebrated in Germany much as in other countries, though with certain differences of custom. New Year's Day, Easter, and Christmas have always been the Germans' great days, the old-time Christmas being especially joyous, as we have seen in our chapter on Christmas. And much of the old festal feeling still accompanies the day. Children, especially, though their Christmases have all been in the new era, are not allowed to suffer for lack of the old Christmas spirit. The old customs may not be so richly followed as in the past, but neither are they completely gone. Reichs and dynasties rise and fall, but Christmas and other age-old celebrations of the year go on—and the roots of traditions, in church and home, run very deep.

The end of the Christmas season—Epiphany, Twelfth Night, or the Festival of the Three Kings—has always been regarded as highly as Christmas day itself in Germany. Then the tree is lighted for the last time, and the coming of the Three Kings is observed in various ways. The initials of the three Magi (whose names, you will remember, were Gaspar, Melchior, and Balthazar) are marked up over the door, so that the Magi will see them when they come, and protect the house from flood and fire. Children, of course, who seize on any excuse to dress up like somebody else, often go around on that night stumbling over long robes as they try to look like the Three Kings themselves.

The very last night of the year is in Germany not only New Year's Eve but also Saint Sylvester's Eve. The double event provides the occasion for very fine feasting, and the principal dish is carp, "Saint Sylvester's carp," a fish served up with ceremony even in the smartest restaurants. "Saint Sylvester's punch" accompanies it. White wine is usually served with fish, isn't it? But in this case an exception is made, for the punch is a concoction of red wine spiced with cinnamon. It is sweetened and then heated, and it is delicious. After some of this punch, no one minds folding up a scale or two of the carp in a paper napkin and taking it home, as a kind of charm to start the New Year off.

Carnival time, just before Lent, used to have its own very special festivities in different parts of Germany. King Carnival held his Fools' Court practically everywhere, and processions wended their absurd way through the streets. In Cologne the celebration was very elaborate. And in Saxony the old struggle between winter and spring, which has inspired so many folk customs through the centuries, was represented by a mock battle between the seasons, with winter the sure loser. In Munich the day before Lent, Shrove Tuesday, was celebrated with religious dramas dating from the Middle Ages.

The Germans have always been outdoor people, and so they have always made the most of the holidays of the seasons. In the old days the coming of spring meant picnics for everybody. The official opening of the outdoor eating season was Pentecost, or Whitsunday, the fiftieth day after Easter. In the country, cowbells were rung, and city people started at daybreak to reach a green open place for laying down the tablecloth. Another favorite picnic time was the summer solstice, the longest day of the year, which usually comes on the twenty-third of June.

The most wonderful and famous holiday of all was, and still is, the Munich Oktoberfest, or October Festival. This is probably the liveliest, longest, and most colorful folk festival in all Europe, and as colorful now as ever, with its sixteen days every fall of *Fasching* (carnival) and of a vast display of sports, food, dances, costumes, arts, and diversions such as only this ancient state of Bavaria (Munich is its capital) can supply. Old meadows known as the *Wies'n* are the scene of this great gathering together of the traditions and customs of a historical and happy way of living, when for two weeks and two days the whole history of a people is telescoped into one time and place.

Men in time-honored dress and carrying old banners pass by in proud ranks. Long wagons laden with red beer casks are drawn by in slow state, each one led by four brightly caparisoned horses. Women in fabulously full dresses and beautiful headdresses link arms as best they can without knocking their market baskets together, and form a small parade of their own. There is nothing in the way of typical Bavarian food you cannot buy at the markets and stalls. And there is no dizzy risk you cannot take, if you are minded to, on the Munich equivalent of carrousel, shoot the chutes, and flying boats.

It is heartening to find the old Germany un-
touched even in these changed and troubled times.
But it is safe to suppose that even in the less happy
parts of Germany, with the goal of a great new holiday before them—the Day of German Unity—the
people will never let the old ways go.

ITALY

Italy's year is thickly studded with holidays—traditional, historical, and religious. How could it
be otherwise? This long boot-shaped land which
stretches down between the Adriatic and Tyrrhenian
Seas into the Mediterranean is filled with riches of
the past as well as of the present. On this terrain
stood ancient Rome. Here too is the heart of Roman
Catholicism: Vatican City, the home of the Pope, a
city within the city of Rome. And here were all the
proud and vivid kingdoms which only in the middle
of the last century coalesced into one whole. For
present-day Italy, home of art and beauty, which
looks so peaceful to the traveler's eye, was the scene
of ceaseless rivalry and warring until finally in 1861
the first Italian Parliament declared Victor Emman-
uel king of Italy.

Italy's main holidays are New Year's Day, Epiphany, Saint Joseph's Day (March 19), Easter, Easter Monday, Liberation Day (April 25), Labor Day (May 1), Ascension Day, Republic Day (June 2), Corpus Christi, Saints Peter and Paul Day (June 29), Assumption (August 15), All Saints' Day (November 1), Victory Day (November 4), Immaculate Conception (December 8), Christmas, and Saint Stephen's Day (December 26). But there are many other celebrations, some of which have come down through the ages—for instance, April 21, which marks the founding of Rome in 753 B.C. The date is of course legendary, having been established much later in Roman history. But April 21 is a good date for a celebration, well along in spring, and suitable for parades and other outdoor ceremonies.

A holiday which flourished for some years was the Twenty-third of March, anniversary of the appearance of Fascism in Italy in 1919. (The name came from the Latin word *fasces*, bundles of sticks carried as an emblem of authority by the Roman *lictors*, who were the attendants of the chief magistrates in ancient Rome.) The *Fascisti*—often called Black Shirts because of their costume—were a political association organized by Benito Mussolini to combat Communism and Socialism. On October 28, 1922, they marched on Rome and took over the government. Mussolini's dictatorship lasted until 1945 when, at the end of the Second World War, he was killed. In 1946 Italy became a republic.

One can imagine the verve and gusto with which troops were reviewed and speeches made by the Duce, as Mussolini was known, on that twenty-third of March. But although he instituted this holiday of his own, he also made a point of not disturbing Italy's traditional festivities, religious or other. "We have revived and fostered," he said, "all those traditional manifestations which lighten the heart and make the mind healthy." To this end he even set up an "Institute of Leisure Hours," something we would think would be unnecessary in that holiday-loving land, where leisure hours have surely never gone to waste.

At any rate, the new holiday called Liberation Day, on April 25, which marked the country's freeing by the Allies in World War II, amply made up for the Institute, the Twenty-third of March, and all the other signs and symbols of Fascist rule.

Saints' days abound in Italy. Every month has at least one, and sometimes several, and some of them are observed by the Italians in their own special ways. Saint Agnes' Day is the fifth of February, in honor of the Sicilian girl Agnes, or Agnata, who suffered martyrdom. She is believed to ward off fire and pestilence. The twenty-fifth of March, the Annunciation, is traditionally the day when the Angel Gabriel visited the Virgin. For the feast of Corpus Christi, in June, the people make lovely carpets of flowers woven in intricate designs. Several cities are famous for these mosaic floral patterns. June thirteenth is set apart for Saint Anthony, patron of horses, mules, and other pack animals.

The day when the Virgin Mary went to visit her cousin Elisabeth, before the birth of Jesus, is observed on the second of July. Elisabeth, the wife of Zacharias, was also expecting a child, the boy called John, later known as John the Baptist. The fifth of July is dedicated to Saint Rosalia, a nun of the twelfth century; and the sixteenth is called the *fiesta* of the Madonna of Carmine, a Neopolitan saint said to heal various ailments. Her altar is heaped not only with candles but with wax replicas of the parts of the body for which the sufferers beg relief. This festival has been brought over to this country and is observed, with elaborate ceremonies, especially in New York City. Another saint who heals the sick is Saint Roche, whose date is August sixteenth. And on the eighth of September all the girls named Maria look forward to receiving presents, for this is their "name day," the birthday of the Virgin Mary.

We have spoken before of Saint Nicholas as the

patron of children, who brought presents on the eve of his day, December 6. But in Italy Saint Nicholas is also the patron saint of sailors. If they are on shore, they carry his image through the streets. When at sea they have his image on the prow of their vessel, so he may give them a good voyage and a safe return. For who would not want to return to Italy, that beautiful country whose past and present take in almost everything that the human mind and heart can hold?

JAPAN

There is a new holiday in Japan—Constitution Day, May 3. This dates from 1947 when, after the Second World War, Japan agreed to have a democratic government under parliamentary rule. Her other holidays are old, some very old indeed—two of them historic landmarks as important as Constitution Day. The first of these is February 11, the accession of the Emperor Jimmu, which marked the beginning of the Japanese Empire in the year 660 B.C. At that time Jimmu Tenno overcame his enemies, formed a united country, and became the first emperor. The second is November 3, birthday of the Emperor Meiji, which commemorates the beginning of modern Japan. During this emperor's long reign, 1867–1912, feudalism was done away with and the rights of the common man were recognized, Japanese ports were opened to foreign ships, and Japan established contact with the rest of the world. The entire week which surrounds this holiday, filled largely with athletic games and sports, is inspired by the idea of educating the younger generation for modern living.

Of course, the birthday of the reigning emperor is always celebrated too. The democratic regime has not done away with the hereditary rights of the royal family. The date is now April 29, the birthday of Emperor Hirohito. Hirohito is the hundred and twenty-fourth of his line, and his son, Crown Prince Akihito, will be the hundred and twenty-fifth.

Another great traditional national holiday is New Year's. This includes not only the first of January but also the second, third, fourth, and fifth. On the first day everyone goes to the temple to worship "in the four directions," as the Japanese say, meaning to worship the gods of the whole world. In the homes special foods, such as the favorite rice cakes, are prepared. No unkind words must be spoken, no unkind thoughts held on this day. Calls are paid and good wishes exchanged over small cups of saké, rice wine.

The second day is called the Beginning of Work, and business houses open their books for the new year with much ceremony. The third day marks the renewal of court functions; and only on the fifth day does a court banquet and reception really complete the elaborate transition from one year to the next.

There are two spring festivals in Japan. The vernal equinox, March 21, is the true Festival of Spring, with roots so deep into the past that they intertwine with those of Shintoism, the ancient religion. But there is a popular and less solemn holiday on the third or fourth of February called Bean-Throwing Night, which is supposed to bid good-by to winter and to hasten spring. Beans, one of Japan's staples, are strewn about as a symbol of spring sowing. But the precious commodity is not unduly wasted, for no person is allowed to throw more than the years of his age. It is thought that evil spirits will be driven out of the house by this ritual—the connection of winter and evil spirits being a very old idea among many peoples.

Two little festivals for children, one for girls and one for boys, have a charm of their own. The girls have March third and for some reason it is called the Peach Festival, though actually it has to do with dolls. The dolls receive guests very formally, and tea is served. May fifth is the holiday of the boys, when large cloth carps, with mouths wide open so the wind will come in and puff them up to handsome proportions, are hung out to fly from poles—one carp for each boy in the house. The carp symbolizes strength and perseverance, because every year it swims upstream to lay its eggs.

Buddhism came to Japan from China, and it is now the dominant religion in Japan. The first Sunday in April is observed as Buddha's birthday, with elaborate services in the temples. Another religious observance, which would seem to have something in common with the Christian All Saints' Day and All Souls' Day, comes during the nights of the Feast of Lanterns, July 13–15. Then the evening is filled with moving spots of light as bearers of paper lanterns go from grave to grave, sweeping the graves clean and leaving small offerings. Sometimes a bonfire is lighted, to shine on the pathway of the departed soul.

The autumnal equinox is celebrated on September 23 with a service in honor of departed ancestors. The Harvest Festival, on October 17, is a time of dancing and fun; and on November 23 comes the Japanese Thanksgiving Day, the Festival of Niiname-Sai. In recent years this has been combined with a labor day, and is known as Labor Thanksgiving.

The last day of the year, O-misoka, is a frenzied

period of stocktaking and debt-paying, at least for those who are inclined to let things go till the last minute. No one may sleep until things are in order; and, after they are in order, a little celebrating must be done. Food, especially noodles, is set out ready for the dotting of the last *i,* the signing of the last check. These noodles are made as long as possible for they are a symbol of life, and to eat them on this night is a prelude to the morrow's "long life and happiness" wishes. Lights in houses and shops burn late. Sometimes the New Year has already come before the O-misoka celebration is well over. And the Japanese year of delicate ancient ritual, carried into a new and modern setting, begins again.

INDIA

The story of all the holidays of India would make a long book. And that long book would have a long appendix, to explain the different regional calendars under which the holidays are celebrated. Mark Twain once spoke of India as the land "of splendor and of rags . . . of a hundred nations and of a hundred tongues . . . of a thousand religions and of three million gods." This was extravagant language, but not altogether unwarranted, for India is a complex land not easily summed up or put into neat categories. In looking for its holidays, all we can do is to pick up a handful of shells from the myriads washed up by that ancient civilization which goes back, at a conservative estimate, at least five thousand years.

So steeped in legend and folklore is this country that every little town may have its own private celebrations, its own special *mela*, or fair, maybe just for fun, maybe in honor of some god. And from such tiny occasions of merriment, handed down from ancient times, the Indian festal spirit goes to the other end of the scale, with such fabulous and world-famous exhibitions as the durbars, parades of the princes, when elephants are bedecked in gorgeous trappings and the men wear splendid jewels. These durbars were receptions held for native princes by the British governor general before India became independent.

The innumerable time-honored holidays continue, although India, after many years as a British colony, is now a republic and has two new holidays, almost incongruous among the rest, dating from 1948 and 1950. In 1948 August 15 was set aside as Indian Independence Day, and in 1950 January 26 was made Republic Day. The people had been waiting a long time for these occasions. Early in 1947 the British government announced its intention of partitioning India into two dominions, and June, 1948, was set for British withdrawal from the country. August 15 was named as Indian Independence Day. The Union of India became on that date a self-governing member of the British Commonwealth of Nations, and on January 26, 1950, the dominion thus created became a democratic republic. So after forty years of struggle by both Hindus and Mohammedans, who are political as well as spiritual forces, India became free and independent.

More than 85 per cent of the Indian population are Hindus. The Hindu New Year comes about the last of April (because a lunar calendar is used, the date is variable), and this is when the devout make pilgrimages to the River Ganges, or other holy streams, for the washing away of their sins. Others make visits to the temples with propitiatory gifts for the gods.

There are two spring festivals—one serious, the other gay. At one, known as Basant, everyone wears green garments, to match the new birth of green in the spring world. This is the time of beginnings, when many a Hindu child begins the long process of education, starting on his ABC's. The other spring holiday, the Holi or Vernal Fire Festival, comes at the first full moon of spring, usually in March. Bonfires light up the scene in the villages, and boys armed with squirt guns spray colored water—red, yellow, and green—on the passers-by. The more you are dyed, the more popular you are shown to be— for there is no malice in this custom, only a kind of too great affection.

One of the oldest and most typical of the religious festivals is in honor of the second god in the trinity, Vishnu. It comes toward the end of June and is called the Procession of the Car, or Juggernaut, which is another name for Vishnu. The Juggernaut is a fearsome object with no legs and only stumps of arms, and is usually carved out of wood. His triumphal car is over forty feet high and has sixteen huge wheels. The spectators bow as it passes them. After the procession, services are held in the god's temple and food blessed by the priests is distributed.

Brother and Sister Day, a very old festival, comes in August. There are several legends as to its origin. According to one, Yama, the god of death, came to the aid of his sister, Yami, the river goddess, and since that time has always been present at her yearly feast. On this day, brothers and sisters pledge their devotion and exchange gifts. A slightly similar day, though far more important, is when Durga, the Divine Mother and wife of the great god Siva, is honored. This has become a kind of Mother's Day, when human mothers as well as divine are remembered with gifts and visits. Even the sister-in-law has a day when she is especially noticed. This is the January festival called Sankranti, set aside for giving alms to the poor and presents to the family. It may be a dubious pleasure to be remembered along with the charity cases—but still, a present is always nice to get, and even sisters-in-law like to have one once in a while.

There is a charming Festival of Lights, or Diwali, in October, when every doorway and window is bright with candles or lamps. Sometimes fireworks are set off, and trash is burned up in bonfires to symbolize the doing away with evil.

All lands have their feasts of the dead, and India's lasts for two weeks, beginning toward the end of September. Places are laid at the table for the departed spirits who are thought to return during that time, and food and drink are offered them.

One of the most interesting of all Indian holidays is Aiyuddha Puja. *Puja* means worship, and at this time the tool of one's trade, the instrument of one's art or profession, is worshiped as a god—lighted up by candles, bowed down to in thankfulness and prayer. The schoolboy honors his schoolbook, set up on the table or shelf; writers exalt their pens, artists their brushes, gardeners their hoes. Housewives have even been known to venerate their brooms. And sometimes the priest comes into the home and blesses worker and implement alike.

It is not strange that in this land of great variety holidays should be of many kinds. We have mentioned only a few. India has made great changes, and yet most of India is still unchanged. And in the holidays of her diverse peoples will be expressed, perhaps forever, the many strains of her humor, her beliefs, her ancient and imaginative mind.

MOSLEM HOLIDAYS

People of the Moslem (Mohammedan) faith are scattered all over the world. In the year 1957, there were more than three hundred and twenty million Moslems in Europe, the Middle East, Africa, India and Pakistan, and Southeast Asia. The great majority, however, are, and always have been, in a group of Oriental countries that we think of as the original and truly Mohammedan lands. The prophet Mohammed himself was born in Mecca, Arabia, about A.D.

570, and the Mohammedan era dates from the He-
gira, Mohammed's flight from Mecca to Medina in
the year 622. Mohammed died ten years later, in
632.

Turkey, one of the chief Moslem countries, became a republic in 1923, and in the following year
the caliphate was abolished, which meant that
church and state were separated. Up to that time the
sultan of Turkey had been also the caliph, or spiritual leader of Islam (the whole body of Moham-
medanism). The word "caliph" means literally "suc-
cessor," and the sultans were supposedly the succes-
sors of Mohammed.

In 1923 most of the purely religious festivals were
dropped in Turkey, but other Moslem lands and
people observe them as before. Dates cannot be
given exactly since the Moslems adhere to the lunar
calendar, which makes their calendar extremely variable. Their twelve months are Muharram, Safar,
Rabia I, Rabia II, Jumada I, Jumada II, Rajab,
Shaban, Ramadan, Shawal, Zul'kadah, and Zul'-
khijah.

On the first day of the first month the new year is
celebrated. People mingle together in the streets, ex-
changing new year's wishes and small coins, and if
by chance one receives a coin before the wish is

spoken, it is kept as a lucky piece throughout the year. The reason why the spoken word would lessen the coin's meaning is lost forever in the haze of time.

On the tenth day of the first month comes Ashura, which commemorates the end of the Flood and Noah's leaving the Ark. Ashura is the name of a sweetened porridge, or pudding, eaten on that day, and it has given its name to the festival. Noah started this himself, the legend says, telling his wife to make the very best pudding possible, now that the ordeal was over and rations would no longer be so limited. So she concocted a really memorable dish, with all the dates, raisins, figs, currants, and nuts that could be stuffed into it. The test of a good Moslem housewife is if she can make a really delicious *ashura*.

The birthday of the prophet Mohammed comes on the eleventh day of the third month. It is a day of great festivity. In Egypt cannons announce the holiday at sunrise. Everywhere oxen and sheep are roasted whole, so there shall be no lack of meat for everyone. And dervishes perform their strange dances in a mingling of worship and entertainment.

Ramadan, the Moslem Lent, comes in the fifth month and is, as our Lent is with us, a time of penance, prayer, and fasting. But, strangely, it is also a time of festivity; the Moslems fast all day and feast by night. The end of the period is celebrated by a splendid three-day festival, when everybody dresses up and exchanges gifts with friends, and elaborate parades and fairs are often held.

Abraham is the ancestor of the Moslems as well as of the Jewish people, and there is a holiday in the twelfth month called the Feast of Sacrifice in memory of Abraham's readiness to sacrifice even his son Isaac to the Lord. Traditionally every family, if it is in any way possible, sacrifices a ram, a lamb, or a smaller animal, decorating it for the slaughter, and gilding its horns if it is a horned animal. The roasted meat is then distributed to friends and to the poor. The slain creature, an example of the saving power of sacrifice, will reward its slaughterer on Judgment Day by carrying him across the perilous narrow bridge between Heaven and Hell.

Thus, with these brilliant festivals and others the almost fairy-story year of the Moslem world runs its course. The devotion which causes all Moslems to look toward Mecca when they pray lingers with rich sweetness and tradition in their holydays.

A LIST OF UNITED STATES HOLIDAYS

January 1	*New Year's Day.* Celebrated in every state and all American possessions.
January 6	*Three Kings' Day (Epiphany).* Celebrated in Puerto Rico. A church holiday commemorating the coming of the Wise Men.
January 8	*Jackson Day,* or *Battle of New Orleans Day.* Celebrated in Louisiana only, but Democrats throughout the country observe the day with Jackson Day dinners. On this day, in 1815, the United States defeated Great Britain in the Battle of New Orleans, the final battle of the War of 1812. American forces were led by General Andrew Jackson, 1767–1845, called "Old Hickory," later the seventh president of the United States.

January 19   *Robert E. Lee's Birthday*. Celebrated in Alabama, Arkansas, Florida, Georgia, Kentucky, Louisiana, Mississippi, North Carolina, South Carolina, Tennessee, and Texas.
Robert E. Lee, Confederate general, was born in 1807, died in 1870.

Lee-Jackson Day. Celebrated in Virginia. Lee's birthday combined with January 21, the birthday of Thomas J. (Stonewall) Jackson, Confederate general, 1824–1863.

January 20   *Inauguration Day*. Celebrated in the District of Columbia every fourth year. The day on which a newly elected president of the United States is inaugurated. Before 1934, March 4; now January 20 of the year following the election.

January 26   *General Douglas MacArthur Day*. Celebrated in Arkansas. The birthday of General MacArthur, 1880–, commander in chief of Allied forces in the Southwest Pacific, Second World War.

January 30   *Franklin D. Roosevelt Day*. Celebrated in Kentucky and the Virgin Islands. The birthday of Franklin D. Roosevelt, 1882–1945, thirty-second president of the United States.

February 2   *Candlemas*. A Church holyday commemorating the Purification of the Virgin Mary. On this day the clergy blesses candles and distributes them among the congregation.

Ground-Hog Day. A day for prophesying the weather. On this day the ground-hog first comes out of his hole. If he can see his shadow, cold weather will continue for six more weeks.

February 3   *Boy Scout Day.* Observed by Scouts throughout this country and its possessions. The anniversary of the founding of the Boy Scouts of America in 1910.

February 12   *Lincoln's Birthday.* Celebrated in Arizona, California, Colorado, Connecticut, Delaware, Illinois, Indiana, Iowa, Kansas, Kentucky, Maryland, Michigan, Minnesota, Montana, Nebraska, Nevada, New Jersey, New York, North Dakota, Ohio, Oregon, Pennsylvania, South Dakota, Tennessee, Utah, Vermont, Washington, West Virginia, Wyoming, Alaska, and the Virgin Islands. The birthday of Abraham Lincoln, 1809–1865, sixteenth president of the United States.

February 14   *Admission Day (Arizona).* Celebrated in Arizona. The day Arizona was admitted to the Union as a state in 1912.

Saint Valentine's Day. A festival in honor of St. Valentine, a Christian martyr of the third century. The custom of sending love tokens at this time has no actual connection with the saint.

February 22
Washington's Birthday. Celebrated in every state, the District of Columbia, and all American possessions. The birthday of George Washington, 1732–1799, first president of the United States and commander in chief of the colonial armies in the American Revolution.

February
Shrove Tuesday. The Tuesday before the beginning of Lent. Celebrated as the Mardi Gras, with colorful parades, balls, and pageants. The name "Mardi Gras," French for Fat Tuesday, refers to the last-minute feasts eaten before the Lenten fast begins.

February or March
Ash Wednesday. Celebrated in Christian churches as the beginning of Lent.

March 1
State Day (Nebraska). Celebrated in Nebraska. The day Nebraska was admitted to the Union as a state, in 1867.

March 2
Texas Independence Day. Celebrated in Texas. The day Texas declared its independence from Mexico in 1836.

March 6
Magellan Day. Celebrated in Guam. The day Guam was discovered by Magellan in 1521.

| March 15 | *Andrew Jackson's Birthday*. Celebrated in Tennessee. |

March 15 — *Andrew Jackson's Birthday*. Celebrated in Tennessee.

March 17 — *St. Patrick's Day*. Celebrated by Irish-Americans.

March 22 — *Emancipation Day*. Celebrated in Puerto Rico. Commemorating the day that slavery was abolished in Puerto Rico in 1873.

March 25 — *Maryland Day*. Celebrated in Maryland. The day the first Maryland settlers landed in Maryland at St. Clement's Island in 1634.

March 30 — *Seward's Day*. Celebrated in Alaska. The day on which a treaty was signed with Russia transferring Alaska to the United States, in 1867. Purchase price was $7,200,000. Named in honor of Secretary of State William Henry Seward, who negotiated the treaty.

March or April — *Good Friday*. A legal holiday in Connecticut, California, Delaware, Florida, Illinois, Indiana, Louisiana, Maryland, Minnesota, New Jersey, North Dakota, Pennsylvania, Tennessee, Canal Zone, Hawaii, Puerto Rico, and the Virgin Islands. The Friday before Easter.

March or April — *Easter*. Celebrated in every state, the District of Columbia, and all American possessions.

March or April	*Easter Monday*. Celebrated in North Carolina and the Virgin Islands.
March or April	*Passover*. Jewish holiday. Falls in the Jewish month of Nisan, which corresponds with the end of March, or April.
April 1	*April Fools' Day* or *All Fools' Day*. A day when practical jokes are played. Its origin is unknown.
April 12	*Halifax Resolution Day*. Celebrated in North Carolina. The day, in 1776, on which the North Carolina Provincial Congress, meeting at Halifax, North Carolina, adopted the Halifax Resolution, "that the delegates for this colony in the Continental Congress be empowered to concur with the delegates of the other colonies in declaring independence." North Carolina was the first colony formally to declare itself for independence.
April 13	*Thomas Jefferson's Birthday*. Celebrated in Alabama, Missouri, Nebraska, Oklahoma, and Virginia. Jefferson, 1743–1826, was the third president of the United States.
April 14	*Pan-American Day*. Celebrated in the twenty-one countries of the Organization of American States: Argentina, Bolivia, Brazil, Chile, Colombia, Costa Rica, Cuba, the Dominican Republic,

Ecuador, El Salvador, Guatemala, Haiti, Honduras, Mexico, Nicaragua, Panama, Paraguay, Peru, the United States, Uruguay, and Venezuela.

April 19
Patriot's Day. Celebrated in Maine and Massachusetts. The day the Battle of Lexington and Concord, Massachusetts, was fought, in 1775; the first battle of the American Revolution.

April 21
San Jacinto Day. Celebrated in Texas. The day of the battle near the mouth of the San Jacinto River, Texas, in 1836, when troops led by General Samuel Houston, later president of Texas, won Texas from Mexico.

April 22
Oklahoma Day. Celebrated in Oklahoma. The day of the famous "run," or scramble for land, when the "Oklahoma Lands" were opened for settlement in 1889.

April 26
Confederate Memorial Day. Celebrated in Alabama, Florida, Georgia, and Mississippi. The day these Southern states commemorate their Civil War dead.

April
Fast Day. Celebrated on the fourth Monday of April in New Hampshire, the only state to continue the Pilgrim custom of setting aside a Fast Day to ask divine blessing on the newly planted crops.

May 1   *May Day.* Celebrated throughout the country in schools, often with Maypole festivities. In the 1880's and 1890's was celebrated as a labor holiday.

May 4   *Rhode Island Independence Day.* Celebrated in Rhode Island. On May 4, 1776, Rhode Island renounced its allegiance to the British king.

May 10   *Confederate Memorial Day.* Celebrated in North Carolina and South Carolina. The day these Southern states commemorate their Civil War dead.

May   *Mother's Day.* Celebrated on the Second Sunday in May.

May   *Armed Forces Day.* Celebrated on the third Saturday in May. This day has now replaced Army Day, April 6; Navy Day, October 27; and Air Force Day, the second Saturday in September.

May 20   *Mecklenburg Declaration Day.* Celebrated in North Carolina. A declaration of independence from England made by citizens of Mecklenburg county, North Carolina, meeting at Charlotte, in 1775.

May 30   *Memorial Day.* Celebrated in all states (except Alabama, Georgia, Mississippi, and South Carolina), the District of Columbia, and all American possessions.

May
or June

Whitsunday. A Church holiday celebrated on the seventh Sunday, or fiftieth day, after Easter. Commemorating the day when the Holy Ghost descended upon the disciples.

June 3

Jefferson Davis' Birthday. Celebrated in Alabama, Florida, Georgia, Mississippi, South Carolina, Texas, and Virginia. Jefferson Davis, 1808–1889, was president of the Confederacy, or Confederated States of America, during the Civil War, 1861–1865.

Confederate Memorial Day. Celebrated in Kentucky, Lousiana, and Tennessee.

June 11

Kamehameha Day. Celebrated in Hawaii. In memory of King Kamehameha IV of the Hawaiian Islands, who reigned from 1854 to 1863.

June

Children's Day. Observed in Protestant Sunday schools on the second Sunday in June. Initiated in June, 1868, by the Methodist Episcopal Church, and later adopted by other churches.

June 14

Flag Day. Celebrated in Pennsylvania; and observed in all states by a display of flags.

June 17

Bunker Hill Day. Celebrated in Boston and its suburbs. The battle of Bunker Hill, Boston, 1775, in the American Revolution.

June   *Father's Day*. Celebrated on the third Sunday in June.

June 20   *West Virginia Day*. The day West Virginia was admitted to the Union as a state in 1863.

June 22   *Organic Act Day*. Celebrated in the Virgin Islands. The day the United States granted an Organic Act, or Constitution, to the Virgin Islands, in 1936.

June 24   *San Juan Day*. Celebrated in Puerto Rico. The day of the Battle of San Juan, a decisive battle of the Spanish-American War, in 1898. The battle ended in victory for the American troops over the Spanish. At the end of the war, in December, 1898, Puerto Rico was ceded to the United States by Spain.

July 4   *Independence Day*. Celebrated in every state, the District of Columbia, and all American possessions. Commonly called the Fourth of July.

July 13   *Nathan Bedford Forrest's Birthday*. Celebrated in Tennessee. Nathan Bedford Forrest, 1821–1877, was a Confederate general and cavalry leader.

July 21   *Liberation Day*. Celebrated in Guam. The day United States marine and army forces entered Guam in 1944, taking the island back from the Japanese who had seized it in December, 1941.

July 24   *Pioneer Day.* Celebrated in Utah. The day the Mormon pioneers, led by Brigham Young, entered the valley of the Great Salt Lake, in 1847, the first settlers in what became the state of Utah.

July 25   *Commonwealth Day (Puerto Rico).* Celebrated in Puerto Rico. The day Puerto Rico was granted a constitution by the United States in 1950.

Supplication Day. Celebrated in the Virgin Islands; at the beginning of the hurricane season.

August 1   *Colorado Day.* Celebrated in Colorado. The day Colorado was admitted to the Union as a state in 1876.

August 14   *V-J Day.* Celebrated in Arkansas as World War II Memorial Day and in Rhode Island as Victory Day. The day on which the fighting with Japan officially ended in World War II, 1945.

August 16   *Bennington Day.* Celebrated in Vermont. Commemorating the Battle of Bennington, 1777, during the American Revolution.

August 30   *Huey P. Long's Birthday.* Celebrated in Louisiana. Huey P. Long, 1893–1935, was virtually a dictator in his state. He was Governor of Louisiana,

1928–1931, and United States Senator, 1931–1935. He was assassinated in 1935.

September   *Labor Day*. Celebrated in every state, the District of Columbia, and all American possessions. The first Monday in September.

September 6   *Lafayette Day*. Celebrated in eleven states. The birthday of the Marquis de Lafayette, 1757–1834, who volunteered his services to this country in the American Revolution, was made a major general and served on Washington's staff.

September 9   *Admission Day*. Celebrated in California. The day California was admitted to the Union as a state in 1850.

September 12   *Defenders' Day*. Celebrated in Maryland. The day Fort McHenry, in Baltimore harbor, was unsuccessfully bombarded by the British in 1814, during the War of 1812. Francis Scott Key, who was a prisoner on a British vessel during the bombardment, wrote "The Star-Spangled Banner" when he saw the American flag still flying the next morning.

September 16   *Cherokee Strip Day*. Celebrated in Oklahoma. The day the "Cherokee Outlet" or "Cherokee Strip," hitherto occupied by Indians in the "Oklahoma Lands," was opened to settlement, in 1893.

September 17   *Citizenship Day.* Replaced I Am An American Day, formerly the third Sunday in May, and Constitution Day, formerly September 17.

September
or October   *Rosh Hashanah, the Jewish New Year.* This falls in the Jewish month of Tishri, in September or early October.

September
or October   *Yom Kippur, the Jewish Day of Atonement.* This falls ten days after Rosh Hashanah, in the Jewish month of Tishri, in late September or early October.

October 9   *Fire Prevention Day.* The date was chosen because the great Chicago fire occurred October 8–9, 1871.

October 12   *Columbus Day.* Celebrated in Alabama, Arizona, Arkansas, California, Colorado, Connecticut, Delaware, Florida, Georgia, Illinois, Indiana, Kansas, Kentucky, Louisiana, Maryland, Massachusetts, Michigan, Minnesota, Missouri, Montana, Nebraska, Nevada, New Hampshire, New Jersey, New Mexico, New York, Ohio, Oklahoma, Oregon, Pennsylvania, Rhode Island, Texas, Utah, Vermont, Washington, West Virginia, Wyoming, and

Puerto Rico. Also called *Fraternal Day* in Alabama; *Discovery Day* in Indiana, North Dakota, and Ohio; *Landing Day* in Wisconsin.

October 18   *Alaska Day.* Celebrated in Alaska. The day Alaska was formally transferred from Russia to the United States at Sitka, in 1867. The Russian flag was pulled down and the United States flag, with its thirty-seven stars, was raised.

October 24   *United Nations Day.* Celebrated very generally in all states and American possessions, and by all eighty-one countries which are members of the United Nations, for the purpose of informing the peoples of the world as to the aims, purposes, and achievements of the UN. The day is part of United Nations Week, October 20–26.

October   *Frances E. Willard Day.* Observed in the schools, in Tennessee, Kansas, and South Dakota on the fourth Friday in October. In memory of Frances E. Willard, 1839–1898, American temperance leader.

October 31   *Admission Day (Nevada).* Celebrated in Nevada. The day Nevada was admitted to the Union as a state in 1864.

November 1   *All Saints' Day.* Celebrated in Louisiana.

November 4	*Will Rogers Day.* Celebrated in Oklahoma. The birthday of Will Rogers, beloved Oklahoma humorist, 1879–1935.
November	*Election Day.* The first Tuesday after the first Monday in November.
November 11	*Veterans' Day,* formerly *Armistice Day.* Celebrated in every state, the District of Columbia, and all American possessions.
November 19	*Discovery Day.* Celebrated in Puerto Rico. The day Puerto Rico was discovered by Columbus, on his second voyage, 1493.
November	*Thanksgiving.* Celebrated in every state, the District of Columbia, and all American possessions; on the fourth Thursday of November.
December 22	*Forefathers' Day.* Celebrated by various New England societies. The anniversary of the day when the Pilgrims landed at Plymouth, Massachusetts, in 1620.
December 25	*Christmas.* Celebrated in every state, the District of Columbia, and all American possessions.
	American Indian Day. Celebrated on various dates in Arizona, California, Colorado, Idaho, Maryland, Nebraska,

New Mexico, New Jersey, New York, Oklahoma, South Dakota, Utah, and Wyoming. This day is for the purpose of recognizing, honoring, and bettering the condition of the American Indian.

BIBLIOGRAPHY

American Patriotic Holidays, by Clara Boyt. Pageant Press, New York, 1955.

Bank and Public Holidays Throughout the World. Guaranty Trust Company of New York (pamphlet).

Christmas Traditions, by William Muir Auld. The Macmillan Company, New York. Latest edition, 1942.

The Christmas Book, by Francis X. Weiser. Harcourt, Brace & Company, New York, 1952.

The Easter Book, by Francis X. Weiser. Harcourt, Brace & Company, New York, 1954.

Every Day's A Holiday, by Ruth Hutchison and Ruth Adams. Harper & Brothers, New York, 1951.

4000 Years of Christmas, by Earl W. Count. Henry Schuman, New York, 1948.

The Holyday Book, by Francis X. Weiser. Harcourt, Brace & Company, New York, 1956.

New Year, Its History, Customs, and Superstitions, by Theodore Gaster. Abelard-Schuman, New York, 1955.

Special Days, Weeks, and Months, 1957. Chamber of

Commerce of the United States, Washington, D.C. (pamphlet).

This brief listing represents only a portion of the help given the author in the preparation of this new edition. Many other books have been consulted, on certain points, not to mention the invaluable array of encyclopedias and other reference materials in the New York Public Library.

My thanks go also to the organizations which have so generously and patiently supplied firsthand, up-to-the-minute information: I would particularly like to mention the American Federation of Labor and Congress of Industrial Organizations; the German Consulate General, New York, and the German Tourist Information Service; the Jewish Information Bureau, Inc.; the National Council of the Protestant Episcopal Church; the Pan-American-Grace Airways, Inc.; the Pan-American Union, Washington, D.C.; and the United States Committee for the United Nations.

For further reading, the following books are suggested:

The American Book of Days, by G. W. Douglas. H. W. Wilson Company, New York. Latest edition, 1948.

All About Christmas, by Maymie R. Krythe. Harper & Brothers, 1954.

We Gather Together, the Story of Thanksgiving, by Ralph and Adelin Linton. Henry Schuman, New York, 1949.

Festivals U.S.A., by Robert Meyer, Jr. Ives Washburn, Inc., 1950.

Festivals Europe, by Robert Meyer, Jr. Ives Washburn, Inc., 1954.

Great Catholic Festivals, by James Lawrence Monks. Henry Schuman, New York (The Great Religious Festivals Series).

Great Protestant Festivals, by Clarence Seidenspinner. Henry Schuman, New York (The Great Religious Festivals Series).

Red Letter Days, A Book of Holiday Customs, by Elizabeth Hough Sechrist. Macrae Smith Company, Philadelphia. Latest edition, 1940.

The Book of Festivals, by Dorothy Gladys Spicer. The Woman's Press, New York, 1937.

Festivals—Italy, by Frances Toor. Crown Publishers, Incorporated, New York, 1953.

INDEX